PULVERIZING | PORTRAITS

PULVERIZING | PORTRAITS

LYNN EMANUEL'S POETRY OF BECOMING

CAMELIA ELIAS

© Camelia Elias | 2010
Pulverizing Portraits: Lynn Emanuel's Poetry of Becoming

Published by EyeCorner Press, January 2010
ISBN: 978-87-992456-8-0

Design and typography: Camelia Elias
Cover image: Camelia Elias, *Isolde's Philosophy* (oil on canvas)

All rights reserved.
No part of this book may be reproduced in any form, without written permission from the publisher and the copyright holder.

Denmark
www.eyecorner.press

For Manna

ACKNOWLEDGMENTS

This book was composed as a direct response to a demand from readers of poetry. At various conferences on literature, poetry, and philosophy, and presenting on the poetry of Lynn Emanuel, I have often been asked whether my essays were part of a larger work on Emanuel. My answer to that was always in the negative. However, having found myself elaborating on the reason for *not* writing a more sustained study, one that had to do with my conviction that what I was doing was more an activity directed towards pleasing myself, thus suggesting that the work of Emanuel is somewhat special and above the levels strictly related to academic demands – these days mainly to produce something that is 'relevant,' has commercial value, and can sell – I ended up asking myself this question: why not? Why not, indeed, especially since some readers have started anticipating a monograph on Emanuel for the very same reason: namely that here is a poet who is special and worth reading and thinking about regardless of institutional pretensions. My first thanks thus go to these devoted readers for insisting. Then to Emanuel herself. Not only has she supported this project from the beginning, but she also invited me to talk to her. We did it in Berlin some years ago, while visiting cafés and museums. I cherish the way in which Emanuel's thought has enriched my own thinking and I feel privileged to count myself among her friends. Speaking of friends who also possess a high intellectual calibre, my gratitude goes to two very fine poetry experts, Bent Sørensen and Søren Hattesen Balle; without their insightful comments this book would have been poorer both in form and content. Lastly, my thanks go to Manna Hojda, my sister, who is an avid poetry reader and the first to have instilled in me my love of poetry. I dedicate this book to her.

Camelia Elias
Roskilde, January 2010

CONTENTS

Prologuing Portraits | 9

Counter-frames | 29

Becoming | 45

Genius | 59

Divas | 75

Untitled | 91

Portrait | 107

Hegemony | 123

Greeting | 149

Counter-mythologies | 173

References | 183

PROLOGUING PORTRAITS

> ... one has to be in possession of literature.
> —JEAN-LUC NANCY

> Eating is her subject.
> —GERTRUDE STEIN

Creating cultural portraits through poetry, particularly prose poetry, is a modern way of combining cultural awareness with formal approaches to genre and poetics. The practitioner of prose poetry is first and foremost a teacher of poetry, then a critic of poetry, and then a poet as such. This book, which is a first study of contemporary American poet Lynn Emanuel, aims at showing how through activating all three capacities at once, the poet succeeds in creating a tight proximity with her readers who become aware of the value and social relevance of poetry.

Lynn Emanuel is one of the crucial figures in American poetry today. Apart from being a celebrated poet she is also a professor at the University of Pittsburgh where she teaches English and creative writing, an activity which she insists keeps her close to things as they happen. Her three books, *Hotel Fiesta* (1984), *The Dig* (1991) and *Then Suddenly—* (1999) have won various prizes such as The National Poetry Series Award, and her poems have been featured in The Pushcart Prize Anthology and Best American Poetry in 1994, 1995, and 1998.

Emanuel's poetry is significant because it situates itself in relation to current debates about the state of poetry, creative writing in the academia, and the importance of drawing on interdisciplinary approaches to poetry via visual aesthetics, poststructuralist literary and theoretical perspectives, and philosophy. For Emanuel, creating proximity to her readers has a dual function: first, to instruct and inspire, and second, to formulate a poetics of prose poetry as a gesture that shows that poetry is not 'only' poetry, nor the territory of established meanings. For Emanuel, poetry which is neither merely formalistic, nor merely didactic is of a self-reflective nature, but it is not so introspective as to leave no room for acknowledging that inspiration comes as a result of a writer being acutely aware of a reader's presence. If it is not a play of gazes that guides the writing – the poet looks around, registers what and how she sees and then reduces the essence of this perception to form or to the limits that language imposes on perception as form – then, it is certainly a play of gestures that informs the writing process: the poet, by acknowledging the presence of a reader, acknowledges the fact that form without performative content is devoid of its potential to create an insightful and personal experience.

One way of dealing with capturing what poetry does culturally is by creating relevant stories that combine narrative techniques with a lyrical mode in the genre of the prose poem. This genre that is made up by its own internal contradictions – poetry or prose? – lends itself to investigations into what poetry no longer seems to be able to grasp, and what it nonetheless grasps at a cultural and aesthetic level.

The fact that most of Emanuel's poems are written in prose form, even when some of them subscribe more visibly to traditional forms, such as lines, meter, and various sound patterns that rely on the use of alliteration, and other such tropes, indicates that the practitioner of prose poetry situates herself between taking formalist approaches to poetry and teaching poetics.

As much of Lynn Emanuel's poetry pays homage to writers and artists who are keenly aware of the significance of portraying a specific cultural *geist*, this book construes readings of Emanuel's work also against the background of such inspirational figures as Gertrude Stein, Emanuel's father, the painter and former pupil and model of Matisse, Akiba Emanuel, and the philosopher Giorgio Agamben (particularly his work on the politics of gesture). The main questions that spring from considering the interrelation between culture, poetics, philosophy, and the visual arts suggest that poetry is not only a creative act in itself but also a creative politics that maintains its relevance in connection with writing programs in the universities. The book thus addresses the following line of inquiry: can poetry make communicable the implications of a gesture as a means to draw on the reader's experiences as they are being translated into the writer's text? Can poetry create a proximity to that quality in language that has the potential to express and hence represent the 'less-than-human?' Can poetry disclose the role of aesthetic analysis in contemporary culture? Furthermore, writings engaged with proximity, potentiality, and genre in its constitutive form as a performative gesture (and here we have fine examples in modernist poets such as Gertrude Stein and T.S. Eliot) are in part responses to medieval parables and sophistries that reflect the extent to which, and under what conditions, discourse can be said to (have) become a failure (or a success). It is with the modernist writers that poetry has become a conscious gesture towards prose. This gesture has mediated between politics and discourse through the means of a heightened sense of style, and has now taken new forms in contemporary writings.

Within this framework, the book looks at what characterizes contemporary American prose poetry today, namely an intensified awareness of being close to something. Poets such as Lynn Emanuel have been increasingly concerned with making style a performative gesture, that is, making poetry a tool for cultural criticism. More than a poet, Emanuel can be considered a cultural theorist, who combines intrinsic and formal constraints with extrinsic and socio-historical methodologies. Insofar as being close to something also means being close to both the inside and the outside, the container and the contained, beginnings and endings alike, the question of proximity invariably poses itself to Emanuel as a question of appropriation, duality, hegemony, inspiration, potentiality, and portrayal. Can we appropriate genius, or the language of the Other by means of becoming "subgeniuses" or subalterns? Can we understand the duality between craft and critique in the academia by means of emphasizing singularity? Can we avoid hegemony by means of dehumanizing discourse, and thus let others (esp. other species than the *homo sapiens*) speak on our behalf? Through these questions, which combine close textual readings with cultural text studies, the book furthers the debate about what constitutes good teaching material in creative writing programs and suggests ways of practicing creative writing that is always relevant, intelligent, and uncompromising.

Pulverizing Portraits attempts to extract the essence of Emanuel's politics of gesture that is defined by her creating a space in which poetry performs a cultural act in which both the writer's and the reader's experiences are translated into a shared text. The consequence of such an event has implications for the ways in which we respond to poetry as it relates to the recording of personal experience yet in a highly constructed form. I propose that what constitutes the performative element in Emanuel's poems is the idea that experience is form, and that any identification that the reader might make with the 'personal' in Emanuel's poetry will not take place in the personal as such but in the proximity to the personal. Emanuel achieves this proximity by way of strong imagery, which, however, does not rely on the use of metaphor, but rather makes recourse to visual elements, almost of filmic proportions. My claim is that when reading, the reader does not follow an idea as much as she 'sees' what is happening.

The inferences that we make regarding what the poetic inspires us to do call for a consideration of the performative in culture: through the poet's eyes, it is not enough to limit our observations to what is immediately available as public gesture and behavior; reference would also have to be made to the self-understanding of the poet who is involved in the creation of a shared reality. Obviously from the poet's perspective, it makes a difference to know that the reader also knows, or realizes when reading, for instance, the poem "Homage to Sharon Stone," that the writer Gertrude Stein was fat or that the actress Sharon Stone is always concerned with her hair. However, as several levels of intentionality are brought together, it is not always easy to determine what agent is responsible for what action. While this statement may be taken to reflect a certain *noir* aesthetics as it brings in intentional levels of description – and Emanuel was influenced by writers within this genre such as Larry Levis, Donald Justice, Marilyn Chin, and Raymond Chandler – it also suggests that her interest in the *noir* iconography, such as dirt, grime, and lusciousness, all at the same time, extends to concerns with issues of class, money, power, and gender that are obsessive, repetitive, and ultimately improper to what is dictated as proper in a community.

Emanuel's poems, while taking politics through a black and white grinding machine, are also a reflection of the colors of thought that challenge a writer: how to write a book when Italo Calvino and Gertrude Stein have already said and done it all?[1] Repeating Calvino's own black and white aesthetics and Stein's colorful philosophy of form expresses a poetics of the book of poetry that is based on interconnectedness. Yet Emanuel's poems, in spite of their global range of associations, also emphasize the local precisely at the moment when "influences choose the writer" (Svalina, 2002). However, as she observes, the space that she creates in her poetry is not a space of anxiety, but a space of "inhabitation." This idea is central to the poetics of the prose poem that inhabits the borders of its own genre as well as those of its related neighbors: prose, poetry, the fragment, the personal or philosophical essay, and so on.

What conditions inhabitation is both an expropriation of style, as well as a process of becoming, and I suggest that what Emanuel's poems do is make a gesture towards a re-configuration of

---

[1] Lynn Emanuel has generously pointed out what some of the sources of inspiration for her books have been. See here, Mathias Svalina's thought-provoking interview (2002).

both prose and poetry, by allowing each to inhabit the other, each to appropriate the other, each to expropriate the other, and each to pulverize the other. This gesture establishes a matter-of-fact situation that the reader can identify with something other than questions of truth or falsehood that invite to validation, interpretation, or dismissal. What we see is thus what we get. We have an example in a prose poem written in response to the question "What is American about American Poetry?" – formulated by *The Poetry Society of America* and posed to influential poets. Emanuel here clearly addresses the relation of the poet's craft to criticism and the poet's power to destabilize established trends. While she begins with invoking the craft of another literary giant, Edmond Jabès, alongside her father, who was a painter and a powerful creative figure, she ponders on what it means to translate their experiences into her own text. She then continues by suggesting that what the poet must learn is to be fearless in her critique of current ideologies and traditions alike and act out of an independent conviction, which, however, rises out of shared memories that are anchored in a sense for a community. I quote here four stanzas, as they capture the ideas that I am interested in pursuing in this book. These ideas have to do with how we see poetry operating according to a cultural matrix in which what is said creatively enhances the cultural production of discourse, thus illuminating the relationship between discursive action and human understanding: how do we write, how do we speak, how do we think? How do these interrelated dimensions affect our understanding of our own cultural situatedness vis-à-vis the nature of our social affinities?

> Another gray day. I stoop again to the lathe of the sentence, the wheel turning, turning, noun and verb, subject and object, the

perfect relentless form of it manufactured not by me but by the typesetter, the printer, by the white of the page itself. Currently, I am writing a book which is an allegory about the sentence and the page, an American allegory, an allegory of the village; I speak in an idiom, a dialect of landscape, my allegory won't let me travel beyond the national boundaries, perhaps it will not even travel beyond the boundaries of the island of a few readers. I persist in the myth of my own American anonymity, my hickishness and oaten oafishness. The very thing Poe railed against so brilliantly in his arguments for symbolism I cling to, I nurture into being, and it opens its eye on the page, in the blur of the terminal and stares at me. We look at each other, myself and the grave I have dug for myself.

I am not an internationalist. I find most of the formulations of the literary global village both dull and horrifyingly public. I want secrets, privacy, I want deposits of the inarticulate and incomprehensible, the queer, the recherche, the national. I want tension between and among specific, intact, intractable particularities, not the warm broth of internationalism that is often poured over everything by uniformed translation. All translation is ideological. I am suspicious of American forays into the literatures of other peoples. I am suspicious of how pleasant and accessible these literatures sound in American English, how available, naked, and transparent these "foreign" texts are. And how flabby, finally, my relation to them must be. There is no tension between their language and my own, there is nothing significant to wrestle with, like Jacob with the angel, no strange visitation, there is no tension, only the flaccid moment of familiarity and agreement: the world really is recognizable and friendly and available for my delectation and consumption.

I know enough about the mythologies of America to know how to inhabit one on the page, as I have here. In "real life" I have been reading Rosemarie Waldrop's extraordinary translations of Edmond Jabès and the tension between us, between Jabès and me, is palpable. I cannot receive Jabès except with respectful irony. Jabès writes about the landscape of the word and the page, the black figure on the white field as divine moment, a landscape out of time and place.

But this is America, no one can write about white and black, the page and the word, without also writing about the skin. That's why Jabès seems remote, strange. That's why he's the author I must enter into argument with. His page and his word are mystical, my page and my world are racial. This is America. I am I, the black word on the white page, I am inside that, I is inside me, my finger ruined by the lathe, the wheel, I type with a limp, heavy, soft, heavy, soft, the ruined stump, the severed foot, stalking the keys, stamping down the black word, I am the press, the typesetter, the type, the typist. I am the type, the specimen that is used to type all the others here on the page written inside America. (Emanuel's address to *The Society of American Poetry*; no date & no pagination specified.)

We can think of these lines as Emanuel's attempt to engage her reader politically and consider how literary bonds are created across nationalities, race, and class. As will become apparent in my subsequent readings of her poems, while Emanuel clearly is as American a poet as one might infer – given how she engages and reworks, for instance, the thoughts of the Beat generation poets and the New York school poets – her poetry is also as French as one might think – given how she struggles in composition particularly with the influences of French modernists, such as Jabès. Being an American poet is here contrasted with a lack of tensions rather than a potential that she might become like Jabès if his language would not reach the speaker in a translated and thus mediated form. This is significant. While the quoted passages assert with some degree of certitude the material values of American poetry – down to the typewriter – they do not seem to agree on what kind of immaterial gesture Jabès's mythologies, allegories, and mysticisms consist of. Here, the reader feels the effect of Emanuel's certain uncertainties on her own skin and is thus performatively pulled into the world of images that turn race into "the specimen" that embodies all human potential. The play on the words "type" and "specimen," evoking Whitman, furthermore enhances the proximity that is created between the writer and the reader as the one makes a gesture towards typ(ify)ing the other, and thus draws her into the speaker's specifying the specimen or specificity of her Americanness.

Here I am interested in the cultural and literary implications of the philosophy of the politics of gesture as it has been conceptualized by Giorgio Agamben. For Agamben the politics of gesture does not have much to do with its 'popular' usage, as in "gesture politics" that describes the discourse of lying politicians; nor is it a politics which renders political discourse as a result of cynical, manipulative media spectacle that reflects our contemporary "pseudo-democracy" (Agamben, 2000). The politics of gesture is seen by Agamben as a positive idiom and an alternative to the community which uses gesture as a means to absorb images like commodities. The positive connotation in Agamben's politics of gesture thus has an adversarial function where the popular meaning of the term is concerned insofar as what he distinguishes is not between the wrong or right cultural implications of false gestures and genuine gestures, but between the alternatives that consider under which condition the politics of gesture enables an encounter between signifiers: text and context, writing and culture, human and less-than-human. Gestures, in Agamben's sense, ought to reflect a means without an end, and ought to constitute a community that is not taken for granted. As he puts it: "What unites human beings among themselves is not a nature, a voice, or a common imprisonment in signifying language; it is the vision of language itself and, therefore, of experiencing language's limits, its *end*. A true community can only be a community that is *not presupposed*" (Agamben, 2000: 47; author's emphasis).

The implication of Agamben's thought for literature in general and for poetry in particular is that writing is not so much about communication as it is about communicability. Here the central challenge is how to make communicable, for instance, the separation of the human from the animal, which Agamben argues is based on a "constitutive political act" rather than on anthropological fact (Agamben, 2002: 39). As I shall argue, contemporary poetry writers extrapolate Agamben's thought and ask similar questions regarding what we can and cannot separate when we constrain gestures to genres.

The move from gesture to genre that the poet consciously engages in reflects some choices that she makes regarding mannerism and style. As manner in its archaic meaning indicates making a gesture, and thus a move, style indicates constraint, and thus reflects a stand-still position. One modernist who has challenged the separation of gesture from manner is, again, Gertrude Stein whose practice of creating a tensioned proximity between the poetry that moves and that which 'becomes' movement, between poetry which resembles prose and poetry which 'is' prose has inspired contemporary poets. Poets such as Lynn Emanuel have taken Stein's effort to displace the cultural aesthetics of her time to their own, and hence ask questions that follow Stein's lead: what poetic thinking and gestures contribute to making poetry communicable and experienced as a certain act (a manifesto, a political statement, or a literary act)? It is with the modernist writers that poetry has become a conscious gesture towards prose. This gesture has mediated between politics and discourse through the means of a heightened sense of style, and has now taken new forms in contemporary writings.

One of the central turns in contemporary American poetry thus thrusts the reader into the ambiguous land of prose and its relation to specific cultural manifestations: prose in relation to poetry; poetry as prose, or prose as poetry; poetry in academia; poets as professors, or professors as poets; creative writing as a business and the business of creativity. The rise of creative writing programs in the US in the 70s discloses a deep concern with what it is that is being produced and recorded in creative circles.[2] This concern is also deeply rooted in a desire to see that the results of the creative writing produced in academia are properly situated in relation to the social and human conditions present at the time.

One of the interesting things about writing cultural texts – and prose poems can be seen as prime examples hereof – is the realization that any creative discourse is culturally determined. As creativity was institutionalized throughout the 70s in the form of writing workshops and MFA programs – which now are more popular than ever and have more impact on the social and professional life of students – the link between literary structured-

---

[2] The most recent study that looks at the history of creative writing in the US is Mark McGurl's work, *The Program Era* (2009) in which he takes issue, among other things, with the question of the extent to which creative writing can be taught particularly when the ones who teach it have never tried creative writing themselves.

ness and cultural constructedness was established. The assumption was then that while students are not poets, they can become poets. Their work can take off by virtue of performing writing tasks which are submitted and subjected to criticism. The communal aspect of writing, revising under guidance, and receiving feedback from aspiring fellow students and established poets alike resulted in the actualization of a writing phenomenon which thus primarily relied on reading performances that enhanced even more the relation of proximity between text and context (or writer and audience). As the 'meaning' of a poem was carefully crafted according to its 'function,' it is clear that writing workshops developed their text production in close proximity to the culture that allowed for such a thing to happen.

Some of the wider implications of this book relate to the fact that both lay people and academics are becoming more and more attracted to creative writing. Creative writing programs at universities are still expanding as there is an increasing interest in the "politics of narrative" and in using texts as identity tools. The prose poem as a quasi-aphoristic genre lends itself particularly to statements about the general human condition, and is therefore the ideal vehicle for both the poet's project of self-expression, and for the audience's desire to mirror its identities in the words of the poet. Text can thus be seen as culture and culture as text.[3] But writing poetry with the purpose of making a gesture towards a cultural understanding that deals with the creation, interpreta-

---

3 I have dealt elsewhere with the dynamics of seeing text as culture and culture as text in the book series initiated at Aalborg University, *Cultural Text Studies (CTS)*. For further details, see the two volumes of essays in the series: *An Introduction* (2005) and *Transatlantic* (2006), both of which I have been involved in co-editing.

tion, and manipulation of meaning on the one hand, and on the other hand, with establishing a close proximity between creativity and the means of producing creativity (by contextualizing the author/audience relation) is no new thing.

Beginning with leading modernists such as Gertrude Stein, the idea that 'poetry' can only be put into words as 'prose' emphasizes both a shift and a return to the classical thought that poetry, like music and nature, first, has to 'make' meaning, second, it has to 'be' meaning, and third, it has to 'become' meaning. While the first stage emphasizes a proximity between the writer and her intent, the second stage foregrounds a relation between the writer and an audience for whom the meaning that 'is' is presupposed. The third stage highlights a relation between the creative product, the poem, and the interpreter. In critical discourse these stages might be identified in the first case as formalism, in which the poem makes meaning by virtue of its formal elements, such as defamiliarization, when the reader is enabled to see that the poem makes meaning because something strange is at stake; the second case follows the lessons of structuralism, in which meaning lies in a presupposed grammar according to whose rules the reader reads; the third case is a clear example of deconstruction in which meaning is rendered unstable, and fluctuating between hierarchies – here, neither the reader nor the meaning of the text is privileged, yet the interaction between the two situates meaning in a displaced position, thus putting it on a track of forever 'becoming' something else.

Many a writer would identify the state of 'becoming' in writing as being a particularly postmodern phenomenon, yet if the notion of an unknown excess prevalent in poetry and taken to its extreme in prose poetry is considered, then one would have to realize that the notion of becoming indicates a propensity towards generic forms. These forms operate across different periods in a synthetic way by way of proximity: prose is close to the poetic, poetry is close to the prosaic, hence there is a potential that the one becomes the other, that the one displaces the other. What enables such a superimposition of genre upon genre is precisely a surplus, an excess, which brings the 'being' of prose closer to its 'becoming' poetry. As such, the postmodern element in this process is as much pre-modern as it is modern, insofar as it constitutes itself as a contemporary response to what has been and what is a politics of gesture.

In the first chapter of this book I thus propose to situate Lynn Emanuel's work within the literary genre called prose poetry. There has been a growing critical interest in this genre, but despite the fact that in 2003 a collection of prose poems appeared with an introduction by David Lehman defining the field, there are only a couple of book-length studies of the genre, and none focusing on a single author writing prose poems.

The following chapters each frame Emanuel differently by looking at her work, for instance, against the background of modernist writing and art with special attention to her father, Akiba Emanuel, and Gertrude Stein, who can be seen as a literary foremother for Emanuel. Emanuel's personal and writerly identity emerges partly as a development of the modernist tradition and its penchant for high art, and partly as an irreverent and humorous break with that tradition. My discussion of tradition is done by looking at the function of the prose poem as it lends itself to instruction on subjectivity, existentialism, ethics, and pleasure through the transformation of thought into wit, or a return of thought to witty representation. These first chapters also constitute individual readings of Emanuel's three collections of poems: *The Dig* (1984), *Hotel Fiesta* (1992) and *Then Suddenly—* (1999). Here the focus is on such notions as, for instance, potentiality, inspiration, amnesia, and titling. In terms of a more sustained focus on each of Emanuel's works, insofar as her later production employs more vigorously the genre of the prose poem, more attention will be given to *Then Suddenly—* and the latest, *Noose and Hook.* (2010).

In terms of considering Emanuel's engagement with form on a general level, it can be said that her poems have a form close to the aphorism and the aphorism's function in philosophical communication. More specifically, the poems express a philosophy of communicating wit. Her books, while engaging with departures from the modernist preoccupation with the relationship of the poet's language to the observable world, retain an interest in narratives of inspiration. However, although not all of Emanuel's poems are prose poems as such, insofar as they obey the rule of the broken line, her desire for narrative betrays her commitment to the kind of inspiration that relies more on composition rather than imagination. In other words, while her books do not explore the language/world relationship through the form of traditional poems, they do rely on the poet communicating with the reader mainly through the form of the prose poem. Furthermore, the prose poem for Emanuel lends itself to explorations of the proximity of language to the world. This proximity is investigated through various representations of the notion of inspiration. Here, Emanuel performs a double step: away from the modernist subjective crisis and transformations, yet returning or looking back unto what delimits the modernist limit-experience. My analysis considers the modernist concern with genius from Gertrude Stein to John Ashbery. As genius requires a medium for representation, the pictorial canvas is literally seen as the space where combinations across ideas (borrowed and original) can unfold. I thus look at *ekphrastic* representations in Gertrude Stein and develop the idea of notional *ekphrasis* in Emanuel's 'concrete' poems. Particularly details, such as Gertrude Stein being a fat woman looking like a typewriter with a dress, are addressed in the context of Romantic inspiration.

Contemporary poets writing in the genre of prose poetry gather their inspiration from their close relationships with their audiences – they often do readings which are followed by comments from the audience. These comments serve as grounds for revisions in subsequent poems. The prose poem thus signals a shift in the relationship between audience and poet. Unlike some modernists (Eliot), who were convinced that only some people were well enough educated and thus capable of understanding high art, poets such as Lynn Emanuel believe that everybody in an audience has the potential to make valid comments which ultimately say something about certain cultural manifestations in society. Poets like her are thus at the foreground of a benevolent postmodern revaluation of American poetry as a voice mediating between artist and audience, enabling both parties to grow from the exchange.

The book concludes with addressing the prose poem as a cultural text which consolidates the idea that culture, as it is played out in contemporary poetry, is about the interplay of differences within the organization of structures. Yet this organization is in turn undermined by both literary and extraliterary discursive practices. Doing cultural text studies means focusing on processes that emphasize the play between experience and modalities of experience, or how experience gets to be translated into text, which is to say that the questions asked invariably address the issues of what is at stake right here and now, and what *becomes* what *is* right here and now. Thomas Carlyle's maxim in which he defines culture still captures the dynamics of this creative movement: "The great law of culture is: Let each become all that he was created capable of being" (Carlyle, 1827: 23).[4] This definition lends itself to modernist endeavors that place emphasis on composition rather than reconstruction in language, and suggests that 'becoming' is at the height of cultural transformation. But not any transformation. For example, it has been said of Gertrude Stein that she had no quarrel with either culture, history, or the self, as Eliot, Joyce and Yeats did. As W. F. Dupee put it:

> Culture in her terminology becomes "composition," an aggregate of institutions, technologies, and human relations that the artist, as artist, accepts as it is, eliciting its meanings primarily through

---

4   In an interesting study tellingly titled, *In Bluebeard's Castle: Some Notes Toward the Redefinition of Culture* (1971) George Steiner continues such traditions as carried on by literary figures such as Carlyle, Arnold, Ruskin, and Leavis for whom culture and anarchy counterbalance each other precisely in a process of one (culture) becoming the other (anarchy). Advancing the claim that we live in a post-culture era, Steiner proposes that we need to relate to any theory of culture a theory of barbarism (29), thus anticipating some of Agamben's thoughts in philosophy and postmodern thoughts such as Emanuel's in poetry, for whom the internal relations between the structures of the inhuman are of equal importance for the way in which culture puts forth and advances the production of its own aesthetics through proximity to the "barbaric." For Steiner, the demand for considering the "dark" places in literature in close proximity with "culture" is clear, as passing them by would leave no room for "a serious discussion of the human potential": "Art, intellectual pursuits, the development of the natural sciences, many branches of scholarship flourished in the close spatial, temporal proximity to massacre and the death camps. It is the structure and the meaning of that proximity which must be looked at" (30).

eye and ear rather than through mind, memory, or imagination. And words like the other materials of the literary medium, become useful to the artist, assume a character purely aesthetic, in proportion as they can be converted from bearers of established meaning and consciousness association into plastic entities (Dupee in Stein, 1962: xii).

Emanuel's interest in the poetry of becoming, which is all about creating compositions out of culturally loaded composite characters (a subversive and double-edged move), quite appropriately takes its cue from such apt cultural theorists as Carlyle and Stein, and instead of developing solutions as means to an end regarding new reconstructions of form and language, she sets out to make distinctions that situate the unstable features of verbal aesthetics within their cultural milieu. My argument will thus be that in pulverizing portraits, especially those of the "bearers of established meanings," Emanuel illuminates cultural aspects of 'the-very-thing-that-happens' kind, both in their temporal and spatial dimensions. The commitment to the potential in the idea of 'becoming' is here seen as a strategy for a cultural practice that has *being* on the move, and in close proximity to *becoming*.

What attracts me to Emanuel's poetry is the fact that while she can be said to offer the most insightful comments on the state of poetry in the US today – and for that matter anywhere else – her desire is to remain anonymous. Several of her poems, not only submit to this desire but they also testify to it. And why is this so? And how is this compatible with the notion that a writer must make an impact, judging from the now standard formulations that publishing houses use in connection with the publication of anything? One senses that what is at stake in Emanuel's poetry is how to make a gesture towards saying something forceful against the cult of the visible that is linked precisely to such demands that target not the quality of the impact but its commercial, blockbusting potential. According to this potential, writers have to make themselves more visible, show more virility, and act more independently. In Emanuel's poetry one can trace a critique of this sad development that aims at getting writers to publish more rather than think more. Due to this line of argument, *Pulverizing Portraits* deliberately resists offering a synthesis of what can be termed "Emanuel's thought;" it resists turning her ideas into a traditional monograph that sounds like a textbook, or an introduction to this or that. Rather, *Pulverizing Portraits*, aims at allowing for the emergence of Emanuel's ideas as they do in their interrelations, in their establishing connections across genres and genders, readers and restrictions, being and becoming. Here, I intend to demonstrate not only aspects of the dynamics of cultural practice, but also show how performing readings of as yet unpublished texts can be seen to contribute to the idea of pulverizing traditional and surpassed thoughts through destabilizing hegemony, and through didactic instruction.

The last chapters of this book thus deal with Emanuel's work in progress. First I offer a reading of a set of three poems that led Emanuel to her latest work, *Noose and Hook* (2010). Although these texts are not in the public domain, I find it rewarding to pursue a thought in the making, particularly as it proves some of my points regarding creative writing that draws on academic training and that also 'happens' within the academia.

The book thus concludes precisely with performing a moment of *becoming*, as a gesture towards a more sustained opening of the creative impetus that the academic writer, who is also a poet *par excellence*, is capable of.

COUNTER-FRAMES

Poetry is an orphan of silence.
The words never quite equal the experience behind them.
—CHARLES SIMIC

Lovely snipe and tender turn, excellent vapour and tender butter, all the splinter and the trunk, all the joy in weak success, all the joyful tenderness, all the section and the tea, all the stouter symmetry.
—GERTRUDE STEIN

The prose poem, like the fragment, initiates its claim to existence in oxymoron. Yet in spite of the clear antithesis between the notion of prose and that of poetry, most critics have already decided that the prose poem is a genre in its own right. Pointing to the time when the concept of prose poetry was first used, namely in 1869 by Baudelaire in his celebrated *Paris Spleen* or *Petits Poèmes en Prose*, Michael Riffaterre labels Baudelaire's endeavor as being concerned with "the literary genre with an oxymoron for a name" (Riffaterre, 1983: 117). This definition is itself a framing of Baudelaire's own description of what he was doing, namely writing something which, although it seemingly possesses "neither head nor tail" in its form, content-wise "everything in it is both tail and head, alternatively and reciprocally" (Baudelaire, 1968: preface). Riffaterre thus started a chain of definitions of the prose poem that pragmatically situate the prose poem somewhere between prose and poetry[1]. As David Lehman's "Introduction" in his anthology *Great American Prose Poems from Poe to the Present* (2003) shows: "The prose poem is a *hybrid* form, an *anomaly* if not a *paradox* or an *oxymoron*" (13). Brooke Horvath's essay "Why the Prose Poem?" (1991) has an inherently pragmatic agenda: he presents us with nine theses each targeting the prose poem's form vis-à-vis its content. Whatever the prose poem loses at the level of form – the line, rhythm, meter – it gains at the level of content, a special form of 'sayability,' and intimacy with the reader. In a subsequent article, "The Prose Poem and the Secret Life of Poetry," Horvath adds one more thesis to the ones developed earlier, and seems to suggest, again, that whatever is mediated between form and content also constitutes the background of the prose poem's pragmatic function. Not only is the prose poem "especially well suited to pursuing modernist and postmodernist agenda," but it is also capable of formulating itself as "a poem that hides its poetry" (Horvath, 1992: 13).

Horvath's assumptions are based on the observation that the prose poem is free from the constraints that characterize the two genres that the prose poem both separates and brings together,

---

[1] Attempts to define the genre have been made prior to the definition that critics such as Riffaterre offer, yet Riffaterre's definition goes beyond descriptions of the prose poem as such taking into consideration the poetic function of the paradox inherent in the prose poem. Rachel Galvin mentions other critics whose definitions are worth considering: Joris Karl Huysman's "the osmazome of literature, the essential oil of art; George Baker's Loch Ness analogy: "a creature of whose existence we have only very uncertain evidence," and Suzanne Bernard's "Icarian art." (Galvin, 2004: 47)

namely prose and poetry. This freedom is linked to the idea that the prose poem seems to also enjoy the status of behaving like a fragment thus offering "a means of saying the no-longer sayable as well as the as-yet unsaid, thus providing a home for various sorts of fugitive (unpoetic) content, an agenda enhanced by the form's fragmentary nature and marginal status" (12-13).

These generic crossroads point, however, to a problem of nomenclature, as neither of them obeys strict frames of references. The prose poem can be considered a fragment and a fragment a prose poem insofar as they are not something else (the prose poem is not prose because it is a poem, to the same extent that the fragment is not a complete text, yet can be read as a totality because it is self-enclosed (inclusive)). Thus the paradox that the prose poem contains is a paradox of function. That is, even though one has not said anything yet about the form of this genre, one begins to identify its functions. And one of the functions of the prose poem is to formulate a rhetoric of the frame which is able to counter the idea of description (poetic or narrative alike) in prose poetry. I see this rhetoric of the frame as the poet's rhetoric of narrative. The practitioners of prose poetry want to transcend the rules of narration by framing narrative and its constraints. Thus the idea is to undo both narrative and prose, undo the poetics of prose through the poetics of prose poetry.

Anthologies of prose poems, such as Lehman's, work more on the basis of description when it comes to defining the genre, and while some functions of the prose poem are being identified, none of them explain the role of the frame in a prose poem. Lehman's paraphrase of Suzanne Bernard's work from 1957 illustrates this point. It is for instance apparent that when Lehman mentions Bernard's "four requirements" that the prose poem has to fulfill in order for it to qualify as a prose poem, he is actually talking about four frames of functionality, namely, that the prose poem has to "embody the poet's intention," it has to have "an organic unity," it has to "be its own excuse for being" and "it has to be brief" (19). I would suggest then that each of these frames contains an element of agency that transcends the descriptive mode.

Now, if we look at several other definitions, we shall note that the prose poem is not only at odds with prose and poetry but with the very idea of constraint. I would suggest here that while these definitions take liberties with the very act of defining, they indirectly point to the necessity to see the prose poem not merely as an accident of inter-generic concepts, but as a well construed form with a certain set of constraints. For example, commenting on Gertrude Stein's prose poetic style in *Tender Buttons*, Stein being the mother of the American prose poem *par excellence* according to Lehman, Russell Edson in a gesture simultaneously celebratory and frustrated throws up his hands with the comment: "Heck, one can call most anything a prose poem. That's what's great about them, anything that's not something else is probably a prose poem" (in Lehman, 2003: 20).

In one of his several paradoxical and self-referential definitions of the prose poem Charles Simic offers what amounts to a prose poem in its own right: "The prose poem is a result of two contradictory impulses, prose and poetry, and therefore cannot exist, but it does" (14). In another (more prosaic?) definition he establishes a tension between frames and paratexts: "The prose poem is a burst of language following a collision with a large piece of furniture" (19). In "Cold Calls" (2000) Tyrone Williams enacts Simic's definition and performs a prose poem that consists of footnotes and endnotes to a non-existent text (in Lehman, 2004: 247-253). In Williams' case the footnote is a clear example of a paratext informing a frame that both counters and frames the frame consisting of a blank page. James Richardson's sequence of prose poems from 2001 are fragments that he identifies in the title as aphorisms, yet simultaneously in the subtitle he frames them as being "ten-second essays" (218-222).

My aim here is not to extend the existing definitions of the prose poem but to investigate the relationship between the prose poem, what frames it, and what the prose poem itself seems to frame from a generic duality point of view. Judging from the definitions I have offered here, I would suggest that what defines a prose poem is a counter frame to what defines a fragment in its paratextual mode. In prose poems we have a sequence of competing unifying frames with the two genre labels colliding at an intersection: the text is a poetic expression, and yet this expression turns out to be "framed" by the status of the text being in prose. These unifying frames clash with the subversive counter frame of the fragmentary genre that constitutes the prose poem in general and the paratext-driven prose poem in particular.

The question of counter frames imposes itself in some of the already mentioned prose poems that present themselves as fragments of frames of both prose and poems. In other words, while they offer themselves as free from the constraints of ideology inherent in narrative and poetry alike, they are not free, nor do they want to be free from producing poetic effect via poetic intent. This point is emphasized in Steven Monte's book on the prose poem in French and American literature, *Invisible Fences* (2000). Monte laments the over-debated revolutionary character of the prose poem which has given priority to the notion of the "subversive" quality of the formal freedom of a prose poem instead of focusing on the effects that the prose poem has on its readers precisely when constraint itself is being considered. As Monte puts it:

> Constraints can be thought of not only as restrictions to freedom or, conversely, as restrictions that enable freedom, but as generic signals that inform interpretation. If readers of prose poetry have been or become less aware of the genre's constraints, it is perhaps because so much rhetoric surrounding the prose poem has to do with its formal freedom. Or it may be that the illusion of no constraints is itself one of prose poetry's generic traits.
> (Monte, 2000: 8)

Monte calls this situation an "invisible fence" that not only surrounds the prose poem, but also frames it as a problem à la John Ashbery. "All right. The problem is that there is no problem" ("The Recital"), says Ashbery thus echoing the potential of a prose poem to present itself as an 'as if genre,' as an 'as yet genre,' and as a consequence of a genre that is in between acts of constitution. In other words, the prose poem is not only an oxymoron, but a problem of logical lyric.

In his book *The American Prose Poem: Poetic Form and the Boundaries of Genre* (1998) Michel Delville points to the ideology of genre whose objective is to register literary movements. Following Adena Rosmarin, for whom "a genre is chosen or defined to fit neither a historical nor a theoretical reality but to serve a pragmatic end" (Rosmarin (49-50) in Delville), Delville makes the assumption that the pragmatic charge involves a registering of formal movements. The movement from poetry to prose and from prose to poetry marks not only the instability of genre, but also the fact that incompatibilities exist between forms of poetry and forms of narration. He writes:

> The retrieval and revaluation of forgotten, minor and marginal genres, the preoccupation with intertextuality and pastiche, and the desire for cross-cultural and cross-discursive forms all testify to a new network of complications, contradictions and paradoxes not easily containable within the symmetrical hierarchies and paradigms of traditional genre theories. In the midst of this postgeneric chaos, the prose poem remains a relatively young genre still in the process of self-definition, a formal abstraction whose changing methods and ambitions are exceptionally difficult to define and formulate. (Delville, 1998: 9-10)

Considering the nature and function of the prose poem, it is clear that while its nature relies precisely on distinguishing between the frames that constitute and contain prose and poetry separately, the function of the prose poem is to erase that distinction all together. Hence the prose poem's oxymoronic status. Thus, while frames institute and maintain the incompatibility between prose and poetry, the fact that the prose poem exists, as Simic pointed out, suggests that whatever is subversive about the genre is directed to 'setting up' the frame that aims at keeping things separate. Frame the frame, as it were. We find an example of a frame that sets up its own mode of representation in the often-quoted passage from Coleridge: "the proper and immediate object of Poetry is the communication of pleasure... I wish our clever young poets would remember my homely definitions of prose and poetry; that is, prose: words in their best order; poetry: the best words in the best order" (Coleridge, 1836: 45). Insofar as one can never decide which words are best, as was shown so masterly by Gertrude Stein for whom words do not have a symbolic reference, one is bound to regard words as objects in their own right. Thus, stripped from its symbolic adornment poetry becomes naked prose. If this new form puts on new clothes, the dress will ideologically express the fashion of the time.

The implication of seeing the prose poem from an ideological point of view is linked to the idea that a genre exists in relation to other forms[2]. A new genre frames the cultural manifestations that make it a genre in the first place, and lets itself be framed by a number of features that distinguish it from other genres. There is thus an interdependent relationship between form and content and this is where the notion of the fragment comes in.

The fragment, as its Latin root suggests, is a radical form of breaking. However, the fragment is as problematic a genre as is the prose poem, insofar as it has been defined mainly according to either a period (Romantic, Ancient, etc.) or according to aesthetic or generic terms (philosophical, literary). To make a long debate extremely short, perhaps I could suggest that whatever the fragment's nature – a detachment or ruinous form – in terms of its function, the fragment has always been regarded as a footnote to the idea of totality or complete text[3]. With the German Romantics, however, the fragment has shifted position, from incompleteness to completeness. The fragment has been shown to

---

[2] Ideology is often linked to politics when it comes to defining the genre of prose poetry, as works such as Jonathan Monroe's *A Poverty of Objects: The Prose Poem and the Politics of Genre* (1987) show. What is emphasized is "the struggle" between modes of poetic manifestations. As Monroe puts it: "The prose poem is that place within literature where social antagonisms of gender and class achieve generic expression, where aesthetic conflicts between and among literary genres manifest themselves concisely and concretely as a displacement, projection, and symbolic reenactment of more broadly based social struggles" (Monroe, 1987: 18).

[3] I have dealt with the subject of the fragment more amply in an earlier study, *The Fragment: Towards a History and Poetics of a Performative Genre* (2004).

counter the rhetoric of a narrative frame that granted a complete text – a text that has a beginning middle and end – more authority. It is thus through a writer's justifications that the fragment has become a genre in its own right, and it is still evolving, yet this evolution does not take place according to generic and discursive conventions, but develops as a gesture towards self-labeling. In other words, the fragment, like the prose poem is not concerned with what and how conventional generic frames determine its status, but with a justification of the why, and hence why not? Once the question "why the prose poem" is posed – the title of Brooke Horvath's essay, for example – one can proceed to asking another question instead of providing an answer, namely one that implicates the rhetoric of the frame as it is, simultaneously, ideologically constrained and free from ideological constraint. Thus, why not the prose poem?

American prose poem authors such as Lynn Emanuel have already anticipated the discourse of counter-frames in poems such as "The politics of narrative: Why I am a poet," echoing Frank O'Hara's poem "Why I am not a painter." In Emanuel's poem the distinction between prose and poetry is meant not to bridge the polarity between the two but to separate the waters that run underneath. Featuring a conversation with the poet Mark Strand, Emanuel's speaker informs us that she "cannot stand to write prose," identifying prose with tedious descriptions where authors write lines such as "the draperies were burnt orange and the carpet was brown." In Mark Strand's reply that a poet could do that if that was the only thing the poet did, Emanuel decides that while she can muster strength for "the very beginning and the very end," she does not have "the stomach for the rest of it" (Emanuel, 1999: 18).

Whatever constitutes narrative as a 'full' text rather than a fragment is rendered here as remainder or a residue in plenitude, yet the sort of abundance and excess one can easily dispose of. The interesting thing that happens is that the politics of narrative takes the place of a subject's predicate, in the modifications of beginnings and endings. There is a surplus in the very act of subtracting the middle from the beginning, middle, and end formula. This surplus is given to us both as excess, literally and metaphorically through the word "very," and as an expropriation of the proper in narrative. "Why the prose poem?" instead of prose or poetry, is indirectly answered through notions that render the 'why' a matter of in-between-ness.

More directly, the justification implied in the act of explaining the 'why' functions as a poetic manifesto. Insofar as the prose poem does not merely define itself against the background of either poetry or narration, but against the politics of poetry or narration, it establishes itself as a poetics that aims at counter-framing both narrative and poetry. As such it falls between narrative and poetry and constitutes itself as an aesthetic program that mixes thematic levels with genre, context with history, rhetoric with imagism. In other words, the prose poem establishes itself as an oxymoron, yet an oxymoron that is crafted in the image of narration or poetry.

The position of in-between-ness, which the prose poem occupies by countering its own frames of narrative, is also dealt with in Tom Whalen's prose poem "Why I Hate the Prose Poem." Whalen's poetic lines in his prose poem run fast catching up with narration as the following lines indicate: I quote the poem here in its entirety:

An angry man came into the kitchen where his wife was busying herself about supper and exploded.

My mother told me this story every day of her life, until one day she exploded.

But it is not a story, she always pointed out. It's a prose poem.

One day I saw a man feeding a hot dog to his dog. The hot dog looked like a stick of dynamite.

Often simply the sight of a prose poem makes me sick.

I am unmarried and live alone in a small house.

In my spare time, I am cultivating a night garden.
(in Lehman, 2003: 205)

Whalen's prose poem, if it had not been for the way its title frames it, would be a fragment. Not only is the poem self-reflexive, but it is also performative. The mother's story, which becomes a prose poem, explodes the conventions around narrative and formulates itself as a structure concerned with the sentence. Every sentence seems to offer a different structural model. In the first two lines we have a story presented in a straight narrative manner that contains plot, or a narrated event, and time, or a chronological order. The strategy of shifting between discourse and story is maintained throughout the poem. Thus in the third line we are presented with a comment on genre. But, insofar as the third line is also part of a narrated event, genre gets to be translated into narrative. This narrative is however framed by self-reflexivity, which continues in the fifth line, though not before the line is interrupted by a narrative voice similar to the one in the first couple of lines. The poem thus sets up a tension between narration, self-reflexivity, and aesthetic judgment. The question of why the speaker hates the prose poem is framed thematically against the grain of genre. The frame within the frame, the comment on the nature of the prose poem within narrative discourse functions as a story that frames the prose poem and vice versa. Whalen does not just write about the prose poem, or about why he hates the prose poem. He writes a prose poem in the image of prose and poetry. Or a footnote to what separates prose from poetry.

More explicitly on the function of the prose poem as a footnote I can refer to the example of Tyrone Williams in "Cold Calls" where he literally enacts or performs the prose poem as a paratext to the idea of narrative or poetry. The fact that the text proper is missing from the page suggests that the prose poem constitutes itself as an impropriety against the background of the more 'proper' genres (remember Coleridge?). Yet these genres, which Williams' poem only hints at, are shown to be wearing the emperor's new clothes. Formally, while prose and poetry have very exact attributes such as plot, story, tropes, rhymes and rhythms, they are also very naked. Here, I suggest that the prose poem is being denied this very nakedness whenever authors who are more comfortable with the two dominant genres pass aesthetic judgments on the prose poem. These evaluative comments do not have much to do with the prose poem as such. The same goes for authors who define the prose poem as a mere anomaly. More inspired formulations must aim at taking into account not only the paratexual function of the prose poem in relation to other genres (hence the frame) but also the fact that genres are always implicated in the way we 'see' things. We have an example in

Horvath's essay "Why the Prose Poem?" where he makes an analogy to language. As he puts it:

> As any number of linguists have told us, one's language affects how one sees and thinks, consequently *what* one sees and knows. As a subsystem, if you will, of a language, poetry is generated by a double set of rules that exert control over what can be thought [...] To write, then, poetry in prose is to pursue poetry via a different subsystem, a different grammar, in the hopes of thinking new thoughts. (Horvath, 1991: 111-112)

The implication of this statement is the fact that the prose poem is given agency to create, or rather invent, different subsystems. One such subsystem is developed in Williams's "Cold Calls," where the footnotes, in tandem with their correlating end notes, enter a process of triangulation: from prose to poetry via the prose poem. As the first footnote reads:

> The spatial/temporal lacuna insures the possibility of temporary disruption – or permanent abortion – of service, insures only the probability of successful enunciation, its own passing over. Cf. Paul Laurence Dunbar as an example of such disruption, failure, breakdown: "My voice falls dead a foot from mine old lips/And but its ghost doth reach that vessel/passing, passing"[4]. (Williams (from *Hambone*) in Lehman, 2003: 247)

Here we are invited to contemplate the nakedness of the text proper, and literally 'see' through the paratext the stripping of narrative and poetry off their garments. In Williams's use of such words as "spatial/temporal lacuna," "abortion," "ghost," "pass-

---

[4] Williams' footnote is itself footnoted by an endnote.

ing" and "passing over" what is emphasized is not the absence of a proper text that the footnote accompanies nonetheless, but this text's potential to be there even as we do not seem to be able to see it there. Thus Williams's poem is a most ingenious fabrication that plays with the idea of frames and counter-frames on different levels. The more obvious observation we can make is that we can actually see the regression of the footnote take place while it takes place, as it is passed over to the endnote. That is, the footnote itself is framed by an endnote in which we find the reference to Laurence Dunbar's "Ships that Pass in the Night."

The enunciating power of this poem is revealed already in these first lines of the footnote, by letting voice mark a distance: the voice that "falls dead a foot" from the speaker's lips leaves a trace that the ghost follows, as if in passing. And we have several types of distances in this poem: the distance between presence, absence, and virtuality; the distance between seeing, thinking, and formulating; and the distance between the poet's own voice, the speaker's voice, and the voice captured between quotations marks. These triangulations furthermore form the thematic range of the notion of passing explored by Williams in his 13 footnotes and 15 endnotes. "Passing" voice to genre, and genre to the prose poem itself, is dealt with in the same way the notion of passing itself is shown to frame and let itself be framed, as the many associative connotations of the word suggest: passing over, passing away, passing as, passing.

By way of making a concluding remark, then, I want to suggest that the prose poem, by operating with frames and counter-frames, ultimately formulates its own rhetoric of a passing genre. This rhetoric situates the prose poem not so much between prose and poetry, but rather puts it on a track towards interrelations, and beyond formalism and experimentalism. The prose poem is passing as prose poem. The prose poem is a passing prose poem.

BECOMING

To read what was never written.
—WALTER BENJAMIN

The writer is to serve god or mammon by writing the way it has been written or by writing the way it is being written that is to say the way the writing is writing.
—GERTRUDE STEIN

One of the functions of the prose poem, besides its aesthetic look – being all over the place topographically, so to speak – or besides its being an 'inconvenient' genre, is that it lends itself to instruction on subjectivity, existentialism, ethics, and the pleasure principle via employing a certain tone, namely one that is found in witty prose or commentary, packaged, or rather disguised as a certain literary mode, namely that of the aphorism. A common claim regarding theoretical poetics and philosophical investigation is that, at least in theory, it is not easy to find much wit. However, there are theorists who use aphorisms in their philosophical and literary theoretical takes on the formulation of poetics. Here, I am interested in analyzing two types of texts: essays on potentiality by Giorgio Agamben, where we a find a specific construction of aphorisms as a case of wit in literary theory, and prose poems by Lynn Emanuel that express an interest in the aphorism's function in philosophical communication, or more specifically, they express a philosophy of communicating wit.

The underlying premise of this chapter is the assumption that whereas wit is linked to 'performing' knowledge, the aphorism is linked to the discovery of knowledge. I am concerned with the performativity of wit, which I describe as theory's cunning, as well as the aphorism's non-performativity, which I describe as theory's mask. Where the aphorism shows a preference for form beyond any challenge, wit shows a preference for content beyond any challenge.

Descartes sets the pace for subsequent works of literary theory and literary philosophy that we enjoy reading for their aphoristic and witty qualities, when he says, "I advance masked." (in Cole, 1992.25). Bridging the divide between abstract and concrete forms of aphoristic manifestations is a means of "philosophising with a hammer" (Nietzsche), or theorising on literature by "using the purest hammered gold-leaf of language, to place upon the incomplete the seeming stamp of finality" (Fadiman, 1962: 6).

Agamben's essays offer insights into what he calls "the gift of art" as the most "original gift," placing writing, and the writing of wit, among the pleasures of thinking. Agamben's theory of potentiality elucidates the practice of theory in a poetic way that connects to the world, not through poetic meaning, but through signification. For instance, reading poems by Lynn Emanuel through Agamben's prism of potentiality, one arrives at an understanding of the relationship between the realization of self-consciousness and its actualization in estrangement (Agamben, 1999c: 100-101).

Here I argue that Emanuel's poems in her collection *Then, Suddenly—* constitute an archivization of the process of becoming (a poet) through wit, much in the same manner as Agamben's theory constitutes a poetics of being (a philosopher) through aphorism. Both Agamben and Emanuel employ a style through which they mediate between wit and theory, poetry and the aphorism by making recourse to what Agamben calls the expropriation of manner. Agamben's question in his essay of the same title "Expropriated Manner" in *The End of the Poem*, "Why does poetry matter to us?" will here be read through Emanuel's prose poem: "The Politics of Narrative: Why I am a Poet." As Emanuel places emphasis on wit and emotion, when she exclaims: "God I hate prose. I think that the average reader likes ideas," she discloses an instance of "expropriated" mannerism that manifests an "improper" relation of being to becoming (Emanuel, 1999: 18).

The postmodern aphorism, here the latter 20th century aphorism, distinguishes itself from both the French maxims of the 17 and 18th century and the German fragment written by authors belonging to the Jena group in 1790 (such as Schlegel, Novalis, Tieck, and Wackenroder). Unlike the aphorism of these other periods, the postmodern aphorism is characterized by making wit performative. Performative wit interjected into the otherwise neat and often symmetrical construction that characterizes the form of the aphorism is wit that substitutes the necessity for linear meaning with potentiality.

To illustrate this point we can compare three definitions on the aphorism from 1600, 1800, and 2000. We note that while they all seem to follow the French tradition by mimicking the most obvious quality inherent in the aphorism, namely brevity, they make use of wit in different ways when it comes to defining the aphorism both directly and indirectly as that which is something short and often therefore presumed wise. The first one from Samuel Butler's *Observations* reads: "Summaries that contain most things are always shortest themselves" (Butler, 1979). The second aphorism from Nietzsche's *Twilight of Idols* (1888) reads: "It is my ambition to say in ten sentences what other men say in whole books — what other men do not say in whole books" (Nietzsche: 1990: 115). Finally we have an example of a third aphorism that belongs to a sequence of prose poems from 2001 by James Richardson. These prose poems called "vectors," which Richardson nevertheless identifies in the title as aphorisms, emerge simultaneously in the subtitle as "ten-second essays." The aphorism reads: "The road reaches every place, the short cut only one" (Richardson in Lehman, 2003: 218).

In the first two instances it is the provocative statements that deal with the aphorism's rhetorical constitution that express wit. Wit is part of the modality in which the aphorism "enters into a signifier/signified partnership with an 'object'" (Friecke in Bell, 1997: 15). Here the very form of the aphorism performs the function of wit, wit thus being subordinated to form insofar as the call to make it short communicates not a philosophy of potentiality but a linearity of thought that has to follow a certain trajectory. In Richardson's aphorism wit is not performed by and within form but itself performs a function of potentiality. Wit in the postmodern aphorism is not about form as much as it is about framing form.

In Agamben's work we find similar postmodern aphoristic sentences that make recourse to the performativity of wit by defining potentiality in relation to incapacity. For example, Agamben's examinations orbit around the problem with names for which there is no definition as they form the foundation of speech. In the essay on Derrida, "Pardes," Agamben tackles what he calls the "White Knight's theorem" based on a Lewis Carroll formula in *Through the Looking Glass*, "the name of the name is not a name." Here Agamben says:

> It is worth noting that this "White Knight's theorem" lies at the basis both of Wittgenstein's thesis according to which "we cannot express through language what expresses *itself* in language" and Milner's linguistic axiom, "the linguistic term has no proper name." In each case, what is essential is that if I want to say an *intentio*, to name the name I will no longer be able to distinguish between word and thing, concept and object, the term and its reference." (Agamben, 1999: 213)

Agamben rewrites the gnomic sentences of Caroll, Wittgenstein, and Milner by implying that the literary quality of the modality in which we express ourselves through language, through the naming of the name, has to pass through different potential states. What Agamben is saying is in fact very similar to Richardson's aphorism. Every *intentio* is the shortcut that leads to one place only, which is to say that language has to maintain its relation not with what we can actualize when traveling the narrow road, but with making potential realize in actualization the divide at the crossroad between word and thing. Says Agamben:

> To be potential means: to be one's own lack, *to be in relation to one's own incapacity.* Beings that exist in the mode of potentiality *are capable of their own impotentiality;* and only in this way do they become potential. They *can be* because they are in relation to their non-Being. In potentiality sensation is in relation to anaesthesia, knowledge to ignorance, vision to darkness. (182)

Agamben's discourse on potentiality is remarkable as it lends itself to the understanding of mechanisms that render language significant in its banal mode, true in its deceiving significations, and open-ended in its concealed meanings. Agamben's performative wit comes to the fore in his questions:

> But what is the relation between impotentiality and potentiality, between the potentiality to not-be and the potentiality to be? And how can there be potentiality, if all potentiality is always already impotentiality? *How is it possible to consider the actuality of the potentiality to not-be?* The actuality of the potentiality to play the piano is the performance of a piece for the piano; but what is the actuality of the potentiality to not-play? The actuality of the potentiality to think is the thinking of this or that thought; but what is the actuality of the potentiality to not-think? (183)

For Agamben wit manifests itself when it frames the form that language takes in spite of itself. Insofar as for some writers the aphorism makes people write, Agamben's questions suggest some pertinent solutions for justifying the position that poets such as Lynn Emanuel assume. Emanuel situates herself potentially as a writer whose enunciations cannot be dissociated from the system of her foundational statements that she makes in relation to being a writer who actualizes her potential. For Emanuel, being a writer is about transforming the potential to tell a story into an abstraction that would tell the story for the writer. Potentiality for Emanuel means disengaging from concepts that merely rely on form instead of function.

The collection of poems *Then Suddenly*— researches the idea of combining wit with its potential to not-be. Potentiality is suggested already in the title as if intending to expropriate language of its poeticized terminology. I am interested in expropriation, not in its common usage of depriving of property, but in its more archaic form that indicates the voluntary renunciation of property or propriety, the *proprius*, one's own (self). For Emanuel wit manifests itself at the level where not being a certain kind of writer, here a novelist, opens up to not-being one who becomes one. Her prose poem "The Politics of Narrative: Why I am a Poet" is an example. The poem opens with statements that shift between potential metaphors that realize a poem and narrative strategies such as the actual telling of a story. The speaker finds herself at somebody's house where she is introduced to a male person whom she is supposed to become better acquainted with, at least according to her friend who facilitates the encounter. Emanuel sets out from the beginning to tell a story that the reader reads not for its poetic language but for its narrative grip. As soon as another story is mentioned as part of the main story frame, the reader's hermeneutic desire is aroused and we find ourselves reading for the plot:

> Jill's a good kid who's had some tough luck. But that's another story. It's a day when the smell of fish from Tib's hash house is so strong you could build a garage on it. We are sitting in Izzy's where Carl has just built us a couple of solid highballs. He's okay, Carl is, if you don't count his Roamin' Hands and Rushin' Fingers. Then again, that should be the only trouble we should have in this life. Anyway, Jill says, "Why don't you tell about it? Nobody ever gets the poet's point of view." I don't know, maybe she's right. Jill's just a kid, but she's been around; she knows what's what.
>
> So I tell Jill, we are at Izzy's just like now when he comes in. And the first thing I notice is his hair, which has been Vitalis-ed into submission. But, honey, it won't work, and it gives him a kind of rumpled your-boudoir-or-mine look. I don't know why I noticed that before I noticed his face. Maybe it was just the highballs do-

> ing the looking. Anyway then I see this his face, and I'm telling you – I'm telling Jill – this is a masterpiece of a face.
>
> But – and this is the god's own truth – I'm tired of beauty.
> (Emanuel 1999: 16)

The story becomes more and more intense, both at the level of telling – to us and the other protagonist – as well as the level of showing not just descriptively but also contemplatively the consequences and implications of the meeting. However, half way through it, the speaker interrupts herself with meta-conscious statements on the value of story telling, the position of the storyteller vis-à-vis the reader (or listener) and the nature of conceptualizing language and writing. Emanuel's discourse here makes us aware of the fact that what we have been reading up until this point is not prose, nor poetry, but rhythms, words, cadences, and an attempt to versify the generic love story into an aphorism. The expropriation of narrative, or rather the politics of narrative, occurs at the point when searching for meaning is introduced. In search for something to say, when Jill initiates a topic by encouraging the speaker to tell: "Nobody ever gets the poet's point of view," the speaker throws the story off its track and says:

> And here is where I say to Jill, I just can't go on. I mean how we get from the smile into the bedroom, how it all happens and what all happens, just bores me. I am a conceptual storyteller. In fact, I'm a conceptual liver. I prefer the cookbook to the actual meal. Feeling bores me. That's why I write poetry. In poetry you just give the instructions to the reader and say, "Reader, you go on from here." And what I like about poetry is its readers, because they are giving people. I mean those are people you can trust to get the job done. They pull their own weight. If I had to have someone at my back in a dark alley, I'd want it to be a poetry reader. They are not like

some people, who maybe do it right if you tell them, "Put this foot down, and now put that one in front of the other, button your coat, wipe your nose."

So, really, I do it for the readers who work hard and, I feel, deserve something better than they're used to getting. I do it for the working stiff. And I write for people like myself, who are just tired of the trickle-down theory where somebody spends pages and pages on some fat book where everything including the draperies, which happened to be *burnt orange*, are described, and, further, are some *metaphor* for something [...] God, I hate prose. I think the average reader likes ideas.

"A sentence, unlike a line, is not a station of the cross." I said this to the poet Mark Strand. (17-18)

The implication of statements such as "I just can't go on," while at the same time going on, alluding to Beckett's certain uncertainty in *The Unnamable* (1953) and referring to the incapacity to go on either with love or the story, is that the process of story-telling is dependent on descriptions and is thus less conceptual. For Emanuel conceptual story-telling engages wit in a process that combines self-consciousness with descriptive estrangement. If a story is too descriptive, dependent on too many metaphors, no expropriation takes place that would make the reader take the road of potentiality. Therefore conceptual story-telling necessarily has to end in an aphorism, such as the one the speaker offers the poet Mark Strand. Emanuel's aphorism furthermore explores the relationship between the discovery of knowledge and the consequent performing of knowledge. Exorcising the descriptive out of narrative is for Emanuel a way of registering the quality of wit in an aphorism. Telling us what a sentence is not, yet by conjuring up a descriptive image of the "station of the cross," is for Emanuel a reinforcement of the intertexts that we find present in any aphorism.

Here, *Then Suddenly—* offers a paratextual level in the use of epigraphs. These epigraphs taken in conjunction with the ones Emanuel herself makes up during a poem offer a shortcut insight into the many places that Emanuel's conceptual roads lead to. An example is the epigraph from Gertrude Stein to the book's Part 3: "Think of narrative from this thing, a narrative can give emotion because an emotion is dependent upon a succession upon a thing having a beginning and a middle and an ending" (45). What Emanuel does, then, in Part 1 of the book, is anticipate bridging the gap between form and content, knowledge and the discovery of knowledge, by putting description on hold, by expropriating the manner of telling for the sake of appropriating the style of engaging philosophically with wit and knowledge. Thus, aphorisms for Emanuel do not have a rhetorical quality inherent in them; they have an expropriated quality to them insofar as wit in her aphorisms acts as a free agent.

As examples of conceptual thinking, Emanuel's aphorisms are not concerned with length, they are concerned with style. Insofar as the very idea of a prose poem in itself is an oxymoron, as we have prose and poem both combined and yet running counter to each other, framing each other, Emanuel seems to follow in Agamben's footsteps who asks the question: "Why does poetry matter do us?" (Agamben, 1999b: 93). As Agamben suggests that conceptual thinking is the very thing that mediates between manner and style, his question becomes the beginning of a politics of gesture. Lynn Emanuel's 'political message' – renouncing prose – and address to the reader – whom she trusts to like ideas rather than descriptions – comes at the point when the speaker declares her incapacity to go on with something she dislikes or sees as redundant, thus again throwing into potentiality conceptual thinking itself. The declaration that she cannot go on with the narrative becomes itself an aphorism that expropriates the manner in which the consequence of that telling constitutes the poet's experience as manifested through the style that wit assumes. In this case the only proper gesture that is left to the poet to make is towards creating an archive of styles that would catalogue notions such as appropriation and expropriation.

Conceptual thinking needs an archive whose spectral function, to follow Derrida[1], is to make potential the actualization of narration as aphorism. The aphorism is thus the manner through which the style of narration is expropriated from its conventional seat. The aim of the poet then, by drawing on the reader's experience, by trusting the reader to understand concepts in a concentrated form rather than in a developed form through platitudes, which narration enables, is to instruct on what the bottom line is in any matter, whether of existential or aesthetic proportions. The poet acknowledges in the reader's assumed presence her capacity to reflect back the spectral image of a poetics, rather than politics, of narrative that the poet throws at her.

For Emanuel, the gesture towards creating an archive of ideas consists in the identification of aphorisms with the poet herself.

---

[1] Says Derrida in his *Archive Fever* in which he discusses Freud's postulations as theses that can be archived in the idea of substitution, or here expropriation: "the structure of the archive is spectral. It is *spectral a priori*: neither present nor absent "in the flesh," neither visible nor invisible, a trace always referring to another whose eyes can never be met" (Derrida, 1995: 84). Similarly, for Agamben the spectrality of concepts manifests itself as potentiality whereas for Emanuel it is a philosophy of becoming.

Wit that is performative must mediate between the passages from the beginning and the end, or the passages from expropriation and appropriation, which the poet, unlike a prose writer, wants to skip. Emanuel's aphorisms constitute a shortcut to the kind of expropriation that distances manner from style. Telling the poet Mark Strand what she cannot narrate, the speaker of Emanuel's poem ends up dwelling in expropriating the proper in the act of telling:

> I said: "I could not stand to write prose; I could not stand to have to write things like 'the draperies were burnt orange and the carpet was brown.'" And he said, "You could do it if that's all you did, if that was the beginning and the end of your novel." So please, don't ask me for a little trail of bread crumbs to get from the smile to the bedroom, and from the bedroom to the death at the end, although you can ask me a lot about death. That's all I like, the very beginning and the very end. I haven't got the stomach for the rest of it. (Emanuel, 1999: 18)

Thus, to be able to expropriate the proper and appropriate the improper is Emanuel's road that leads to many places. These acts constitute the postmodern aphorism and its aim to frame form and content and consequently settle in transformation. The search for strategies to become a poet instead of being a storyteller, the search for becoming a conceptual storyteller is by making wit potential in relation to its actualization in the aphorism.

For both Agamben and Emanuel, the conceptualization of philosophy as a shortcut to potentiality as the one place that yet opens up unto the road that leads to many actualizations (in Emanuel's case of narrative in poetry, in Agamben's case of poetry in narrative) manifests itself in a concern with poetic expression that expresses the 'not-being' case of poetry. Where Agamben's essays deal with the textualization of wit in the aphorism on theory, Emanuel's prose poems communicate a philosophy of wit in the theory on aphorism. Although neither wit nor aphorism is mentioned as such in their works, Agamben's and Emanuel's ideas lend themselves to interpretations that render wit the potential that actualizes aphoristic language. I argue that this language is the language *par excellence* of the prose poem insofar as the prose poem situates itself trans-generically also between different modes of conceptualizing what ultimately poetry can teach.

The aphorism that has wit not in a subordinated position, but in a position of free agency, manifests the expectation of the impossible in philosophy, namely stating its own praxis of thinking. Communicating philosophy is the expropriation of thinking when one takes into consideration the "vectors" of potentiality. These vectors mark the actuality of the potentiality to not-think (Agamben), or not-narrate (Emanuel) in the aphorism whose wit is performative. Insofar as we can contend that potentiality marks none of the stability characteristic of the "proper," the process of becoming a poet, for Emanuel, presupposes engaging didactically, first, with offering descriptions of a poetics of being a philosopher. For Emanuel, then, poetry is the space where narration is the actuality of the potential to not-narrate. For Agamben, the inclusion of the proper within the space of the improper constitutes a moment of identifying the place of poetic language and its actualization in the space of the improper. This is what Agamben calls the "gift of art" that situates philosophical wit and aphoristic language among the pleasures of thinking.

For Emanuel, the implications of thinking across potentialities for formulating a poetics of poetry that has creative writing and how to do it as its primary aim is that by allowing various genres that go into programmatic creative writing to fluctuate between prose, poetry, the aphorism, or the fragment, she opens up a space for more than self-expression. Thus the implicit affirmations "I do" (poetry), or "I am" (a poet) formulated against the background of conceptual heuristics become not only distinguishably performative, but also examples of the way in which poetry can be said to achieve its astonishing quality. Ultimately what philosophers interested in the politics of gesture, such as Agamben, and what poets interested in the politics of narrative, such as Emanuel, tell us, is that the very thinking of oneself as a philosopher or as a poet is already a miracle in itself if what is achieved is an exchange and complete compatibility between self-expression and other-expression. One begins to understand what Arthur Rimbaud meant with his famous "I is another," a phrase that bypasses programmatic modes of subject constitution via creative writing and into considering what another's creative genius can establish for the poet whose work, if any good, is bound to remain in a state of actualizing its own potential via communicating older forms of wit and wisdom.

GENIUS

(Inside IS – so wonderful.) (The book that follows is inside her.
It is maybe even her womb itself.)
—HÉLÈNE CIXOUS

As long as the outside does not put a value on you it remains outside but when it does put a value on you then it gets inside or rather if the outside puts a value on you then all your inside gets to be outside.
—GERTRUDE STEIN

Some poets believe in genius. Although the notion of genius has assumed various forms and meanings throughout history – such as divine inspiration and a guiding spirit in the Middle Ages, wit or the natural ability of the mind to produce new thoughts in the Romantic period, and impersonality and the authority of tradition in modernist times – genius today, when referred to in connection to poetic expression, embodies old meanings as well as new meanings. For some poets, being a poet is first and foremost a question of genius work: how to arrive at new combinations, how to make them work, and how to make them acknowledged. In her poem from 1999, "inside gertrude stein," Lynn Emanuel contemplates what it is to be a "subgenius" engaged in depicting a portrait of the genius Gertrude Stein. To Emanuel it is not enough to have the creative genius juxtapose, compare, and confront literary strategies for poetic expression; the genius must at all times be "inside" someone else. It is clear from the beginning that Emanuel relies in her poem on at least two meanings of the notion of genius: "to beget" and to be "guided." Inside Gertrude Stein the speaker of the poem assumes two positions: listening to Gertrude Stein's calling and waiting to be begotten by Gertrude Stein herself. Using repetition, Stein's master trope and literary device in her writings, Emanuel thus initiates a sexual prelude to the intercourse with Gertrude Stein's poetry through *ekphrasis*. In Peter Wagner's definition: "Consisting of the prefix 'ek' (or ec and even 'ex') meaning 'from' or 'out of', and the root term 'phrasis', a synonym for the Greek *lexis* or *hermeneia*, as well as for the Latin *dictio* or *elocutio* (the verb *phrazein* denotes 'to tell, declare, pronounce'), *ekphrasis* originally meant 'a full or vivid description'" (Wagner, 1996: 12).

In Emanuel's poem there are two types of *ekphrasis* at work: notional and actual. First, Emanuel begins with idealized descriptions of a Gertrude Stein portrait that does not exist. In her depiction of the inside of Gertrude Stein, Emanuel also portrays herself insofar as she sees herself begotten in the image of Gertrude Stein. We have an instance of what constitutes notional *ekphrasis* in the first lines:

> Right now as I am talking to you and as you are being talked to, without letup, it is becoming clear that gertrude stein has hijacked me and that this feeling that you are having now as you read this, that this is what it feels like to be inside gertrude stein. This is what it feels like to be a huge typewriter in a dress. (Emanuel, 1999: 13)

Emanuel's insisting that this is what it feels like to be inside Gertrude Stein, without actually letting us know what 'this' refers to, is a way of conceptualizing the notional idea behind Gertrude Stein without explaining the actual Gertrude Stein. Then Emanuel goes on to making references to a real portrait, namely Picasso's portrait of Gertrude Stein thus mixing actual *ekphrasis* with notional *ekphrasis*. Notional *ekphrasis* is a convenient subcategory of *ekphrasis*, insofar as it has no actual painting it can engage with. Yet unlike actual *ekphrasis* that has also been defined as "the verbal representation of visual representation" (Heffernan, 1993: 3), notional *ekphrasis* operates with portrayal with words and it relies on an illocutionary act on the part of the poet.

When Gertrude Stein wrote on Picasso, she named the resulting text a portrait, so it is a portrait, at least as far as her own articulated perception of it is concerned. In support of her nominal creation, so to speak – nominal in the sense that her prose poem is named performatively as an intended 'literalization' of a mode of seeing with a brush and a canvas as tools for representation – Stein uses cubist writing techniques to thus convey an image of Picasso. However, Picasso's image is not representational, but a series of repetitions that deal with what comes out of Picasso. Stein thus uses the original meaning of *ekphrasis*, namely to declare, to pronounce, and perhaps in this context even to beget. In Emanuel's rendition of *ekphrasis*, this is what she extracts from being inside Gertrude Stein when she further asserts, alternating between the first person singular and the first person plural:

> Yes, I feel we have gotten inside gertrude stein, and of course it is dark inside the enormous gertrude, it is like being locked up in a refrigerator lit only by a smiling rind of cheese. Being inside gertrude is like being inside a monument made of a cloud which is

always moving across the sky which is also always moving. Gertrude is a huge galleon of cloud anchored to the ground by one small tether, yes, I see it down there, do you see that tiny snail glued to the tackboard of the landscape? That is alice. So, I am inside gertrude; we belong to each other, she and I, and it is so wonderful because I have always been a thin woman inside of whom a big woman is screaming to get out, and she's out now and if a river could type this is how it would sound, pure and complicated and enormous. Now we are lilting across the countryside, and we are talking, and if the wind could type it would sound like this, ongoing and repetitious, abstracting and stylizing everything, like our famous haircut painted by Picasso. (Emanuel, 1999: 13)

Literally contrasting her own tiny size to that of Stein leads the speaker to conclude that her being a "subgenius" is primarily a consequence of what is *not* there. There is not enough of her for depiction, or to fill a canvas. In the absence of body fat and solid appearance one thus must make recourse not to words but to voice and to seeing. Thus, the notional *ekphrasis* that we get of Gertrude Stein's genius in Emanuel's poem is realized by references to both actual and notional *ekphrasis* that Gertrude Stein performs in her portrait of Picasso. Stein creates a *tableau* that makes Picasso's genius perform intercourse with the depicted subjects, including herself. Emanuel's being inside, becomes for Stein a pulling outside, as the following lines indicate:

> This one was having always something being coming out of him, something having completely a real meaning. This one was one whom some were following. This one was one who was working and he was one needing this thing needing to be working so as to be one having some way of being one having some way of working. This one was one who was working. This one was one having

something come out of him something having meaning. (Stein, 1967: 214)

Insofar as something has definitely come out of both Stein and Picasso, and intercourse has taken place between writing and seeing, the verbal and the visual, one could argue that the method of real and notional *ekphrasis* is performing instaurations of several *tableaux* of geniuses. The orgasmic goal of Stein's and Emanuel's poems is to celebrate the intercourse between the (sub)genius creators and the reader of the poems. Here I am interested in seeing how Stein's poetic genius, which insists on conceptualizations whose clarifications are given not literally but visually, gets transmitted both to poets such as Emanuel, and the reader. Stein's poetic gesture, which both reveals what it intends to depict while at the same time withdrawing the depicting pen from the depicted counterpart, constitutes an *ekphrastic* moment that contextualizes the reader's understanding of her concepts in a concatenation of seeing and telling rather than writing and listening.

Gertrude Stein's poetic genius in works such as *Look at Me Now and Here I Am* – a work that combines writings and lectures written between 1909 and 1945 – comes to expression in her refusal to offer the reader any conceptual examples. In the book's two sections on "Portraits of Objects" and "Portraits of People" Stein's preoccupations are not with exemplifying and describing concepts. What she is interested in is the reproduction of concrete details that she repeats and insists upon with the purpose of creating contextualized conceptualizations. By situating concepts in a specific context, yet without exemplifying how these concepts are to be imagined, Stein creates an *ekphrastic* framework for the protection of her genius. *Ekphrasis*, as James Heffernan has it, "originates in the Homeric story of a shield designed precisely 'to protect / What it advertises': the Greek way of life" (Heffernan, 1993: 174). Critics and poets such as John Ashbery have noted that Gertrude Stein's writing, which is a string of one affirmative statement after the other, is difficult to argue with, precisely because of its consecutive series of ideas (Ashbery, 1989: 108).

One does not argue with poetic conceptualizations that are both self-portraits and self-reflective. One could however argue that Stein's own excitement about her genius – which, to the extent that it was accepted by others close to her, was accepted on faith rather than true acknowledgment – worked as a protection shield which ensured that the newness in her writings stayed that way, namely, fresh, new, and brilliant. Commenting on Picasso's paintings and how they achieved perfection, Stein also makes a remark regarding the inherent paradox in the concept of the modern, namely that as soon as everybody recognizes a work to be good and original, the adventure of either genius or originality is over. Thus Stein consciously situates her writing in a context that transcends modernism by foregrounding her concepts, first visually and only then literally.

Few have been able to understand how Stein's masterful hand can pictorially withdraw from the depicted object, which is herself, thus protecting her writing from its own self-revelations. As Ashbery further remarks, Stein's portrait of Picasso is in reality a portrait of herself. Thus what Stein means to say with her string of considerations of what is to come out of the creative process, namely, something however undefined, is that the poet must remain true to the project that has the pulverization of received ideas as its aim. Granted, while her writing insists that there is nothing new under the sun, hence the endorsement and use of excessive repetition, what it suggests precisely through repetition is that if 'something' is new, it is so precisely because it is something. Such a tautology emphasizes the constructedness of ideas as strings of connections, but does not rule out the possibility of genius taking place outside of such a string. In fact, the condition for the existence of genius, is, for Stein, the being outside.

Of course, as a writer in exile, one is familiar with the condition of being an outsider, as one is never anything but outside everything, yet, from a formal point of view the position of the outside as that which creates an inside is interesting to consider within the framework that yields 'something,' both as an instance, but also as a result of what remains after everything is said and done. This 'something' can be understood as excitation, or *ec-citation*, a modality through which genius is excited by means of *ex-propriating* other forms. Through dispossessing herself of the self, as it were, becoming a genius by being another, the poet succeeds in excogitating new things and leaving them unexplained as a means of shielding off against interpretation. Yet, while some have problems understanding genius, they often point precisely to what separates the genius from the subgenius. While the genius discovers what is not there, the subgenius invents categories that come out of what is not there. We have the example of Gertrude Stein's brother, who in spite of having enough cultural competence to recognize valuable artistic work, refers to the work of both his sister and Picasso in negative terms. Ashbery quotes Leo Stein:

> "Both he and Gertrude are using their intellects, which they ain't got, to do what would need the finest critical tact, which they ain't got neither..." and again, speaking of the triangular noses in Picasso's *art nègre* figure paintings, "When once you know that a nose is not a nose is not a nose you can go on to discover what all the other things are not..." (110)

The fact remains that in spite of Leo Stein's criticism, both Picasso and Gertrud have achieved notoriety, yet as Ashbery asks, "who has really understood or explained away those noses" and how many people have actually read and gotten anything from *Tender Buttons?* It can be contended that going on to discover all the things that are not there is one main characteristic of how notional *ekphrasis* operates.

One of the most important things that Gertrude Stein has achieved in her works is to secure her genius through and against repetition, pointing to the simultaneous impossibility and necessity to write masterpieces. Through repetition she distinguishes between conceptual examples and contextualized concepts. She explains in her essay "Portraits and Repetition:"

> The thing that is important is the way that portraits of men and women and children is written, by written I mean made. And by made I mean felt [...] Then also there is the important question of repetition and is there any such thing. Is there repetition or is there insistence. I am inclined to believe that there is no such thing as repetition. And really how can there be. This is a thing about which I want you to think before I go on telling about portraits of anything. (Stein, 1967: 99-100)

Stein's essay is both a comment on the importance of repetition and insistence, and a comment on the use of repetition in earlier works in particular *The Making of Americans.* The essay is an explanation of her method without making recourse to examples. While telling us how in *The Making of Americans* she had written on every kind of men and women, the description of men and women as such is not given as an *exemplum* but as a resemblance with something else that seems to exceed categorization, at least gender-wise. This is Stein's way of combining writing as a craft with 'making' poetry as an aesthetic activity whose aim is to capture an age, a *zeitgeist*. As such 'making' becomes devoid of pure emotion and also as such opens a space for a certain kind of cognition, namely that which has the possibility of knowledge of a culture in sight.

Gertrude Stein was one of the first writers who truly understood the relation between writing and culture. But she also understood that every new era that seeks to formulate a new formal language meets resistance. One way in which she dealt with such resistance was to propose a poetics of creative writing as a converging manifesto. What she was interested in, and succeeded in doing, was precisely to establish a relation of nearing the finite point of a contemporary culture. Being, in other words, neither too far from the things that happen right then and there, nor too ahead of her time, Stein served to show that being contemporary means being able to represent not only the contents of one's own head as an inspired poet, but also the thoughts of others. In an interview with Walter Cronkite in 1935, Steins' desire to stay close to her time, near its converging point, becomes apparent: "A writer isn't anything but contemporary. The trouble is that the people are living Twentieth Century and thinking Nineteenth Century [...] Why the fact was evident up at Hockaday [where she stayed in Dallas]. The girls of from fourteen to seventeen understood perfectly, but their teachers did not [...] You must represent in your work what I call the time sense of your period" (Cronkite, 1935).

As a general rule in her writing, and often also by ways of making references to how other writers perceive her writing through mocking her methods and making fun of her thinking, Stein offers a definition not on portraiture, but on what it means to portray and be portrayed; what it means to embody being a cultural theorist who paints. As she puts it: "the making of a portrait of any one is as they are existing and as they are existing has nothing to do with remembering any one or any thing" (Stein, 1967: 105). Here Stein clearly goes against conceptual examples, yet she moves towards contextualizing concepts in the culture that formulates them anew. By telling us everything about what links portraiture and repetition in context and nothing about how this very context is to be conceptualized, Stein points to a remarkable difference between poetry and philosophy that is found in the difference between gesture as insistence and word as repetition.

In his essay, "Gesture and Word," on the practice of philosophy and the practice of poetry, Carlo Sini draws some distinctions between conceptual exemplifying and contextualized thinking that are similar to Stein's practicing of poetry by making portraits that are not representational as such. Says Sini:

> A poet examines the *exemplum* under a microscope, a philosopher through a telescope. And for a poet there is no such thing as an *exemplum*, but only symbols, something whose meaning cannot be translated into a concept and has to maintain its connection with the sensible expression. In doing so the poet refers to

lived experience directly and not instrumentally. (Sini in Verdicchio and Burch, 2002: 23)

Sini's argument illustrates the implications of the possibility to have a trajectory that goes from lived experience to the word and place everything in an original and emotional context. Gertrude Stein's philosophy of writing is a similar gesture towards using examples to describe objects and people that are neither examples, nor descriptions, but an insistence on words. The major insight here, and one which can be attributed to Stein is that, while formally emotion can be dispensed with, insofar as form itself is not pure nothingness it may contain emotion but let it unfold in such a way so as to take on a different substance. When Stein comments on her own famous line: "a rose is a rose is a rose," which emphasizes how the word "rose" can be made separate from the meaning that it offers, she thus contextualizes a concept without using any examples: "When I said, A rose is a rose is a rose, and then later made that into a ring, I made poetry and what did I do I caressed completely caressed and addressed a noun" (quoted by Van Vechten, 1962: xxii-xxiii).

Here I would argue that Gertrude Stein's practice of poetry is *ekphrastic* in its thrust insofar as it links a detailed philosophy of writing to acts of representing culture by formally constricting it to the creation of an event that exceeds mere description. Having insisted on expressing herself through the use of nouns, pronouns, conjunctions, and verbs, Stein returns to nouns and to naming and thus creates a framework of notional *ekphrasis*. One example of notional *ekphrasis*, which one can contend expresses Stein's intent to describe conceptually the graphics that words possess in their referentiality, can be found in a passage from *The*

Autobiography of Alice B. Toklas. In this book, Stein portrays her own work through the image or graphicity of the words used to describe Toklas's writing on Gertrude Stein. Thus, writes Stein ekphrastically through Toklas:

> Gertrude Stein, in her work, has always been possessed by the intellectual passion for exactitude in the description of inner and outer reality. She has produced a simplification by this concentration, and as a result the destruction of associational emotion in poetry and prose. She knows that beauty, music, decoration, the result of emotion should never be the cause, even events should not be the cause of emotion nor should emotion itself be the cause of poetry or prose. They should consist of an exact reproduction of either an outer or inner reality (quoted by Van Vechten, xxiii).

For Stein, associative simplification, or conceptualization without making recourse to examples is instrumental in her addressing directly what Sini calls "lived experience." The reference to herself as being possessed constitutes for Stein an ekphrastic moment in which what is visualized is her gesture towards insistence. The concept behind this *ekphrasis* is the notion of repetition and its emphatic value. Here a question seems to pose itself: in the making of portraits, in what ways can one insist on the value of emphasis? Stein addresses this issue with the combination between word and gesture and repetition and insistence in mind when she further claims in "Portraits and Repetition" that:

> Once started expressing this thing, expressing any thing there can be no repetition because the essence of that expression is insistence, and if you insist you must each time use emphasis and if you use emphasis it is not possible while anybody is alive that they should use exactly the same emphasis. And so let us think seriously

of the difference between repetition and insistence. (Stein, 1967: 100)

One other poet who has thought seriously about the differences that Stein draws up in respect of grounding the conceptualization of things in a poetic context is, of course, Lynn Emanuel. Being interested in portraits herself, Emanuel is also concerned with how one goes from the depiction of lived experience to still life, the life that a subgenius must experience. Lacking the dynamism of creative power associated with the genius, the subgenius, while creative, must obey the rules of the inside if something is to come out of it. Just as Gertrude Stein connects directly to the world through estrangement, Lynn Emanuel's poems make up a *tableau* of sounds, repetitions, rhythms, and figures.

The prose poem "inside gertrude stein" follows the same cadences that Stein herself is famous for creating. The poem makes use of ungrammatical punctuation, and offers both sentences that deal with actualities and events and affirmative statements that are hard to contradict. The picture one gets of Gertrude Stein's physical size is equally balanced by descriptions of how Stein's physicality works as a container that contains not only its own genius but others' too. Emanuel's speaker's descriptions of Gertrude, whose name she insists on repeating in a non-capitalized form as if suggesting that the proper in Stein is always improper, are the same type of descriptions that Stein offers of Picasso. They are based on telling, and follow the same conversational style that Stein uses when she informs her readers repeatedly that she has something to tell us before she goes on with her subject. Ultimately, of course, both Stein and Emanuel tell us nothing of either. They show, however, the workings of emphasis in the act of telling, and insist that something is being conceptualized and ready to come out, yet not in a representational form, but in a relational form.

Emanuel's poem borrows Stein's gestures towards insisting on words creating a flow of imaginary sounds that both the wind and the river would make if they could type. Typing calls for a certain urgency that escalates in the poem as soon as the speaker can hear Stein's voice calling for a continuation of her work. And the reasoning goes as follows:

> Because someone must be gertrude stein, someone must save us from the literalists and realists, and narratives of the beginning and end, someone must be a river that can type. And why not I? Gertrude is insisting on the fact that while I am a subgenius, weighing one hundred five pounds, and living in a small town with an enormous furry male husband who is always in his Cadillac Eldorado driving off to sell something to people who do not deserve the bad luck of this merchandise in their lives – that these facts would not be a problem for gertrude stein. Gertrude and I feel that, for instance, in *Patriarchal Poetry* when (like an avalanche that can type) she is burying the patriarchy, still there persists a sense of condescending affection. So, while I'm a thin, heterosexual subgenius, nevertheless gertrude has chosen me as her tool, just as she chose the patriarchy as a tool for ending the patriarchy. (14)

Emanuel here sets up relational aspects in her poem that are not merely instrumental for the understanding of the way she receives her calling from Gertrude Stein, namely as a cubist painting that is non-representational. But also the poem has a direct relation to lived experience, and cuts across character relations such as Gertrude and Alice, Gertrude and the speaker, Gertrude and the husband. Typing, for Emanuel, also means recasting the characters into *ekphrasis*, which thus literally means that if anything can come out of things, as indicated by the prefix *ec*, then it is definitely something, as indicated by the root *phrasis*, which, again, means to tell, to declare, to pronounce fully, in other words to offer a literally vivid description.

Emanuel's way of conceptualizing things is similar to Stein's insofar as she also approaches language from a potential point of view. Yet this potentiality is so vividly described that it becomes true and therefore it affords no contest. Here, what Ashbery says about Stein applies to Emanuel as well: "It is impossible to refute a statement made in a poem; poetry is by nature true and affords blanket protection to anything one wishes to say in it. Gertrude Stein is a poet in this sense. Like Picasso, she is *building*. Her structures may be demolished; what remains is a sense of someone having built" (Ashbery, 1989: 110).

As for Stein, then, Emanuel's portraits are self-portraits that depict the notional concept of the self as poet. It is the act of self-portrayal, when the subject is revealed while showing, yet withdrawing the portraying hand, that allows the genius to have intercourse with the subgenius, the poem with its reader, and the typewriter with its flood. Making up concepts without explaining them, and putting them in a relational relationship with one another is both a necessary, but also an impossible task that the poet who insists on words as a gesture towards repeating one's own genius gives herself. In this divide between necessity and impossibility, between concepts and their contextualized counterparts, between gesture and words, genius gives off its most potent virility. What Stein and Emanuel have recognized in poetry is that only excited genius as such can keep us from literalists and realists and thus let narrative not frame us but us frame it.

DIVAS

> *It is 12:20 in New York a Friday*
> *three days after Bastille day, yes*
> *it is 1959 and I go get a shoeshine*
> *because I will get off the 4:19 in Easthampton*
> *at 7:15 and then go straight to dinner*
> *and I don't know the people who will feed me.*
> —FRANK O'HARA

> *How many acts are in it?*
> —GERTRUDE STEIN

Emanuel sees culture as a kernel. In our attempt to understand the world around us – understand that which resists us, the gap between different perceptions of the world as motivated by our different backgrounds – we are often thrown right in the middle of a vortex created by the tension between a search for an authentic self and communicability on a larger scale. "Who am I?" and "how do I communicate who I am?" are central questions that revolve around strategies of characterization. Emanuel's poetry, in its concern with culture, also as a way of extending Gertrude Stein's project, is engaged in making cultural statements that are often based on a link between the self and the other, portrayal and ideas – character portrayal, object portrayal, and depictions of places and personalities. One finds an example of her range in the poem, "Homage to Sharon Stone" (from *Then Suddenly—*) that extends quite literally from Gertrude Stein to Sharon Stone. This poem can in fact also be seen as a prime example of a how a cultural text works in its linking a history of ideas with iconic manifestations of texts and images. Most of Emanuel's poems establish themselves as cultural texts, and as such, as discourses that address several levels of reality: 1) in order for the poems to work communicatively, they have to put into operation and activate the author's and reader's cultural awareness; 2) in order for the poems to make themselves intelligible, relevant, and aesthetic (a tall order for any text), they have to be involved in a deliberate reworking of cultural elements. We never experience culture as something complete or at a distance. Here, the cultural kernel is not just an object that is in the poems, but can be thought of as more of a process of collaboration between the author, poems, and the reader. These levels show the extent to which the author's intent of pulling the reader into her world can be said to change the reader's perspectives that, in turn, rework the interpretations of the poems.

By means of illustrating what culture does in terms of the collaborative, I begin here with a short consideration of the very idea of a cultural kernel.[1] Literally, a kernel is a stone. A hard stone. Or a proper name. Either significantly loaded or one of no

---

[1] I am indebted here to Daniel Thomières who organized a conference at the University of Reims with this very title: *The Cultural Kernel* (2008). The main questions posed by Thomières in his call for papers have inspired the reading in this chapter: "what is the importance of the cultural component when we interpret literary texts, esp. texts coming from another culture? Is there a kernel that will always resist us?"

consequence. On looking at Emanuel's poem "Homage to Sharon Stone," one is invited to read the text not only against the grain of what it proposes, mainly to depict a portrait of Sharon Stone, but also to consider the small and the great, the famous and the infamous aspects of living life such as it is, with moments when one feels one has been hit by stones or smaller pebbles, as it were. Although one may think that this poem would have been better fit for Emanuel's previous collection, *The Dig*, when one considers the telluric connotations that it conjures, one can speculate that there is a direct connection to several types of knowledge acquisition at work in this text: some knowledge happens all of a sudden, creating an illusion of cosmic coincidence, while other knowledge we have to dig for in order to achieve. As befits such a framework of thinking, I allow myself to reproduce the poem in its entirety, thus digging it (up) in all the senses of the word:

> It's early morning. This is the "before,"
> the world hanging around in its wrapper,
> blowzy, frumpy, doing nothing: my
> neighbors, hitching themselves to the roles
> of the unhappily married, trundle their three
> mastiffs down the street. I am writing this
> book of poems. My name is Lynn Emanuel.
> I am wearing a bathrobe and curlers; from
> my lips, a Marlboro drips ash on the text.
> It is the third of September nineteen**.
> And as I am writing this in my trifocals
> and slippers, across the street, Sharon Stone,
> her head swollen with curlers, her mouth
> red and narrow as a dancing slipper,
> is rushed into a black limo. And because
> these limos snake up and down my street,

this book will be full of sleek cars nosing
through the shadowy ocean of these words.
Every morning, Sharon Stone, her head
in a helmet of hairdo, wearing a visor
of sunglasses, is engulfed by a limo
the size of a Pullman, and whole fleets
of these wind their way up and down
the street, day after day, giving to the street
(Liberty Avenue in Pittsburgh, PA)
and the book I am writing, an aspect
that is both glamorous and funereal.
My name is Lynn Emanuel, and in this
book I play the part of someone writing
a book, and I take the role seriously,
just as Sharon Stone takes seriously
the role of the diva. I watch the dark
cars disappear her and in my poem
another Pontiac erupts like a big animal
at the cool trough of a shady curb. So,
when you see this black car, do not think
it is a Symbol For Something. It is just
Sharon Stone driving past the house
of Lynn Emanuel who is, at the time,
trying to write a book of poems.

Or you could think of the black car as
Lynn Emanuel, because, really, as an author,
I have always wanted to be a car, even
though most of the time I have to be
the "I," or the woman hanging wash;
I am a woman, one minute, then I am a man,
I am a carnival of Lynn Emanuels:
Lynn in the red dress; Lynn sulking
behind the big nose of my erection;
then I am the train pulling into the station

> when what I would really love to be is
> Gertrude Stein spying on Sharon Stone
> at six in the morning. But enough about
> that, back to the interior decorating:
> On the page, the town looks bald
> and dim so I turn up the amps on
> the radioactive glances of bad boys.
> In a kitchen, I stack pans sleek with
> grease, and on a counter there is a roast
> beef red as a face in a tantrum. Amid all
> this bland strangeness is Sharon Stone,
> who, like an engraved invitation, is asking
> me, *Won't you, too, play a role?* I do not
> choose the black limo rolling down the street
> with the golden stare of my limo headlights
> bringing with me the sun, the moon, and
> Sharon Stone. It is nearly dawn; the sun
> is a fox chewing her foot from the trap;
> every bite is a wound and every wound
> is a red window, a red door, a red road.
> My name is Lynn Emanuel. I am the writer
> trying to unwrite the world that is all around her. (53-54)

Emanuel's poem here shows how the cultural kernel as that which resists us can be overcome by observing domestic practices. While we may not always understand another culture and thus be able to crack its literary productions due to missing implicit referents and indigent symbolizations, daily routine is something that most of us can relate to. We all have bad hair days. Not only does Emanuel establish a close proximity between herself and her reader, by bringing her reader into her house, but she also collaborates with the reader towards understanding the workings of collective cultural competence. If the kernel resists us, or creates a gap, we go for the nearest association. We will understand something, if it must be through misreading. In considering Sharon Stone, the reader who may not know the famous actress, may be prompted to think of the infamous 70s hit song by Smokie: "Who the fuck is Alice?" (or here, Sharon, Gertrude, Lynn?):[2]

> Sally called when she got the word,
> She said: "I suppose you've heard -
> About Alice."
> Well I rushed to the window,
> And I looked outside,
> But I could hardly believe my eyes -
> As a big limousine rolled up
> Into Alice's drive...
>
> Oh, I don't know why she's leaving,
> Or where she's gonna go,
> I guess she's got her reasons,
> But I just
> don't want to know,
> 'Cos for twenty-four years
> I've been living next door to Alice.
> – Alice, who the fuck is Alice?

If we don't stumble over stones in this song, we certainly get hit by a car. A big car. A limo. Within a cultural context, the first

---

2   In the original version played by Smokie, there is no reference to the f-word. However, whenever they often played the song in Ireland, the audience would shout "Who the fuck is Alice?" when the main line was sung, "I've been living next door to Alice." The band then decided to do a spoof of their own song and insert the line in their subsequent recording of it. They collaborated for this with the foul-mouthed Roy Chubby Brown, a stand-up comedian.

question one may pose here is one of recognition. In other words, to what extent can the reader establish that she and Emanuel share the same cultural competence in terms of recognizing similar situations, iconic texts, or the same set of ideas associated with transtextualities, or the ability of the global text to cross national and cultural boundaries? Thus, is Emanuel thinking of Alice, when she sees Sharon, one would like to ask? Or is she thinking of one of her earlier works, *Hotel Fiesta* (1984), which is all about black sedans and limousines?

"Lynn Emanuel," who also happens to be the speaker of Emanuel's poem, definitely wants to know what Sharon is up to. And she clearly knows who Sharon is. But Sharon is taken out of her context, which makes the act of observing even more significant particularly as it relates to consolidating the condition of all cultural understanding and subject constitution: look first, imitate, and understand later. So Lynn does what any good amateur anthropologist should: observe what's going on. In this poem it begins with her taking a seat: by the window, by the door, by the desk. She positions herself strategically in relation to the objects and people that surround her. The aim is to put something on paper. Encircle. What she notices is that the neighbors are also engaged in their routine, namely, playing the role of unhappily married.

The poem shifts quickly between observations that depict cultural manifestations as they happen and their aesthetic translation into text. Characters in their roles, while taking their roles for granted or accepting them as part of societal constraints, are also in a position to pass judgment on their culture's relentless emphasis on creating sameness. The poem thus suggests that even though we all do the same things, culture itself is a generator of difference. The poem concludes with a desire to "unwrite the world that is all around her," Sharon Stone, and presumably Lynn Emanuel alike, but not before the reader gets to witness "the carnival of Lynn Emanuels" as a composite of another character embodiment expressed in the wish to be "Gertrude Stein spying on Sharon Stone at six in the morning" (53). What this example demonstrates is that we never experience culture as something ineffectual. The assumption is that we learn to distinguish between the internal and external origins of inspiration by standing in close proximity to "actuality," or the very thing that happens while it happens.[3]

As Emanuel's poem writes itself through the metaphors of cracking the kernel and smashing the core-stone, the style that emerges from the collaboration between the poet, her subject, the poem, and the reader, also demonstrates that the act of portraying establishes a close relationship between the verbal and the visual. While the depiction of Sharon Stone relies on creating an image-world for the reader that goes beyond language, the fact that the images conjured up are all context-based and anchored in cultural competence points to the significance of how language works in use and the consequences of its self-referentiality. What we are dealing with here is a poem that expresses not just ideas (as poems often do primarily) but also a conscious awareness of the workings of language in and through time. While we can easily see Sharon Stone diva'ing about in a limo in 1999, we do not in the same breath associate the idea of a diva with the 50s tradition.

---

3 Russell Edson wrote a collection of prose poems, *The Very Thing that Happens* (1964) which influenced a number of poets interested in the relationship between readers, writers and the materiality of power in language.

Emanuel portrays herself as a 50s housewife, mocking the last decade of glamour, and contrasts herself here with another 'housewife' of the new millennium for whom even the chore of curling the hair involves external agency (as Sharon Stone probably has somebody else attending to her hairdo). The 50s housewife is thus recast in the passive role of watching, observing, and ultimately identifying, yet not with the character under scrutiny, but with the character's role. The irony is that the 50s housewife is endowed with double agency: on the one hand, she has to make sure that the status quo is maintained, (she stays a product of her culture: she is a housewife, before she is a writer), and on the other hand, she has the potential to become someone else, precisely because this potential is activated by the writer within the housewife.

The subtle point that the poem expresses is that while Emanuel may not be a confessional writer who writes in the same vein as Sylvia Plath, Anne Sexton, Robert Lowell, Allen Ginsberg, and Frank O'Hara, at the same time she both acknowledges and subverts the long tradition of articulating mundane situations in highly crafted poetic constructions. She brings in literary figures such as Gertrude Stein, whom the reader familiar with either her writings or photos of her will instantly recognize as being situated in the opposite direction of glamour: not thin, no curls, no housewife. The fact that Stein, who was also concerned with craft and composition, as emphasized earlier, and who wrote in a most ordinary language, is here taken as a barometer – as Emanuel would like to hear Stein's confessions about Stone – indicates a performative gesture on Emanuel's part, namely pulling the reader into the image world of 'stone on stone,' and ultimately letting her carve her own inscriptions.

This example points to the way in which language works as a cultural construct, and how it configures the human condition according to a specific aesthetics. Emanuel's poem with its concatenation of language awareness and cultural images is ultimately a poem on portraits, a portrait of a poem, a portrait of a (self) portrait and a poem about itself. In other words, a narrative in verse that is not only a manifestation of, but also a gesture towards cultural understanding.

One of the other implicit messages in the poem that we can extrapolate an understanding from is that where culture is concerned events come and go. What remains are portraits, photographs, and descriptions of people in other media. What connects us to events, either current or the ones that remain distant in the past and thus only have significance for people who have experienced them first hand, is that they remind us of something else. In Emanuel's poem, language itself traverses through these events and is shown to adapt itself easily to new modes of representation. We thus go from the event of writing, in which something must be recorded, to activating a memory about a film with Sharon Stone, or a picture that Gertrude Stein portrayed with words. Thus, what Emanuel suggests is that pictures collaborate to inspire writing, and that writing in turn 'reminds' us of fleeting visual moments.

All these alternative modes or representations that are the result of cultural manifestations following a dominant in a certain time and age – writing, film, music, painting – are furthermore shown to collaborate towards the process of de-mystifying seemingly strange relations. We take seriously Emanuel's advice, not to think of big, black cars as symbols for something, but a quick glance at the way in which her writing shapes itself on the page, shows that her "Symbol for Something" is spelled in capital letters which makes us think that Emanuel's writing betrays her at the very moment its graphical representation takes place. Where this reader is concerned, I cannot stop thinking about the mob driving mysteriously in their black Cadillacs in the 50s, or cruising up and down the famous Liberty Avenue luring the 'working girls' towards them. The depiction of Sharon invites that very association insofar as she is portrayed as being a bit mysterious and distant and as having powers that can activate anyone's 'basic instinct.' Any diva with respect for herself knows how to play the mystery part. Roles are thus played seriously. Actors are generous. Directors are merciless. And bit-players take it all in – and then they write about it.

In Emanuel's poem, the smart move from the trivial associations that we get from linking picture to picture – film to film, song to song, writing to writing – to overcoming the state of 'this merely reminds me of something' is done through bringing in the master who knows a thing or two about strange relations. In her famous book, *The Making of Americans*, written in 1909 and published in 1925, Gertrude Stein repeatedly insists that she writes for herself and strangers. What can culture do in the face of such enunciations, or questions, one is tempted to ask? Or what is the textual cultural practice that enables or conditions the articulation of such enunciations, or questions? What can strangers do for one's writing, and what can one's writing do for them? If we stay with reminiscences, for a while here, we can say that what the democratization of creative writing in the 70s reminds us of is that the practice of disseminating creativity is nowhere more visible than in the practice of blogging on the internet. More than ever technology has enabled what Stein has prophesied. Now the slogan is: 'I blog to myself and strangers.' Thus we associate. But there is nothing new in associating. We associate incongruous events. But there is nothing new in this either. Perhaps it is more interesting. So we associate symbolic events. Yet, while the situation of 'nothing new' presents itself again, we can at least claim self-authorial legitimacy for this or that interpretation. It is precisely at this point that the cultural kernel presents itself not only as a challenge where decoding cultural codes is concerned, but also as an opportunity to break them.

The knack to dealing with the cultural kernel is not in the cracking, but in the playing of parts. Lynn Emanuel finds Sharon's question: *"Won't you, too, play a role?"* attractive. She is a bit-player, like the rest of us. What is suggested in the line immediately before this question: "amid all this bland strangeness is Sharon Stone" is that in the face of remaining speechless in our encounter with the strange, especially the bland kind, or strangers, especially the blond ones, we can start singing our own praises. The picture that Lynn Emanuel depicts of the 'other' Lynn in the poem, the one who is engaged in a very similar writing practice to our nowadays blogging, is suggestive of the kind of impersonations we are capable of in the face of performing. We assign roles to one another and play the parts too by taking turns at being the other. In the following two paragraphs I am tempted to give myself over to essayistic and poetic writing, and emphasize, by shifting registers, the way in which collaboration on a personal level can be entangled with scholarly work. Prompted by Emanuel's intent, to pull the reader into her world, I thus pose the following questions:

What about the third of September? Is that Sharon's birthday? Or Gertrude's? Or Lynn's? Or is it really about the 15th of November when T.S. Eliot went to see Gertrude in Paris, which made Gertrude write that portrait poem that has wool and silk in it? Lynn says Sharon's head is swollen, and Gertrude says Eliot's mouth is woolen. Speech impediment. Or is it about me, having to skip a meeting on the third of March, because I had to bash my brain and write on the writers of dates for the purpose of presenting these very thoughts at the conference on the cultural kernel in Reims? I collaborated too. I let my friend and colleague, a polyglot punster and professor of German, Hartmut Haberland, know that I was finalizing this book, while on my way to France – no pilgrimage on stones – and this is what he gave me: "Gertrude Stein was born on February 3 as so many other good people. (Joyce was one day early, which must have been a mistake. Groundhog day! Who would eat a ground hog? Well, I better mince my words ...) I was always wondering if Alice B. Toklas was a real name or a pun. I hope your topic doesn't leave you speechless. 'Talkless in Reims' sounds like a take-off on 'Speechless in Seattle' (You have my permission to use it.)" And so I do, right here in this medium, to our collective stunning astonishment.

We step around the cultural kernel by looking at the alphabet. Grammar of the stepping-stone. It's all in there: in the stoning of the text. Gertrude says in her *To Do: Book of Alphabets and Birthdays:* "alphabets and names make games and everybody has a name and all the same they have in a way to have a birthday" (Stein, 2001: 5). Groundhog day is here to stay. Baptism day. (P.S. The story doesn't end here. There was a mail from my colleague, one day after he had sent me the above, in which he says: "of course I meant 'Sleepless in Seattle.' Maybe you thought it was intended, and since we are talking about open texts here, who gives a fuck for my intention?" It goes to show that if the cultural kernel resists us, we have a couple of choices we can make, at least where authors' intentions are concerned. The tongue won't know the difference, if it sleeps, slips, or remains speechless.

✣

If we, however, leave such discourse above aside, we can conclude that writing prose poems, or poems that clearly follow a narrative line that draws on readers' cultural competences, has the aim to raise consciousness around a writing practice that faces a challenge where poetic astonishment is concerned. When one, as a poet, is not allowed to conjure any sublime feelings via an embellished discourse in the Romantic or any other tradition – Gertrude Stein was a master at replacing the heart with the head, the narrative line with the sentence – the question that the poet has to confront, is how to create astonishment without betraying the geniuses who have been influential in one's poetic formation. The prose poem, which combines narrative and metaphor almost in equal measure, has the potential to undo the otherwise easily identifiable cultural codes existent in a work that already has the ecstatic, the transcendental, and the political on its agenda. Thus the poems in *Then Suddenly—*, which in themselves can be said to constitute almost miniature examples of cultural studies, question the underlying values of what is always presupposed by others, also in relation to writing. What Emanuel does is thus ask the question: what is the function and value of writing when it is retained to limiting knowledge, when it is constrained to either taking the advice of geniuses, or discarding it, or playing it safe by becoming experimental? What will astonish, in the end?

In their collection of critical essays, *How We Love to Be Astonished* (a title inspired by the poetry of Lynn Hejinian) Laura Hinton and Cynthia Hogue propose that art itself, the writing of experimental poetry, can question the cultural relevance of art. Following Marjorie Perloff's seminal study of postmodern poetry, *Radical Artifice: Writing Poetry in the Age of Media*, Hinton and Hogue argue that the modernist formal concerns with language and innovation, which can be traced in the avant-garde postmodernist poem, are tightly interlinked with postmodern cultural practices that acknowledge culture as a result of processes of hybridization and crossings of thresholds and boundaries (Hinton and Hogue, 2002: 4). This point is made even more succinctly by Perloff, whose text is used as an epigraph to Hinton and Hogue's introduction:

> Whereas Modernist poetics was overwhelmingly committed, at least in theory, to the "natural look," [...] we are now witnessing a return to artifice, but a "radical artifice" [...] less a matter of ingenuity and manner, of elaboration and elegant subterfuge, than of the recognition that a poem or painting or performance text is a made thing – contrived, constructed, chosen [....] At its best, such construction empowers the audience by altering the perceptions of how things happen (1).

For Emanuel, this particular project of showing not only how a poem is made, but also what it teaches, has another aim at its heart, as well, formulated in the question: what to call it, this thing that happens, the acquisition of knowledge, that is? And how long does it take us to get there, to knowing things? And then finally, what do we do with our new perceptions that thus change due to new knowledge?

Here one is tempted to say that perhaps there is a reason why Emanuel took almost a decade between her collections of poetry. There are, for instance, fifteen years between *Hotel Fiesta* and

Then Suddenly— but there is something that links these works: fixed and fluid connections. Metaphorically speaking, while the vehicle for the transportation of knowledge remains the same, the limousine, the way in which the limo cruises, from the dusty streets of Ely Nevada in *Hotel Fiesta,* to the metropolitan streets in *Then Suddenly*—, is reminiscent of the desire to see shadows incarnate. In *Hotel Fiesta*, beginning with the epigraph: "Let dust remember," the figures of the father, Mark Rothko, Jews in Berlin, Grandmother in Tunis, Hamlet and the ghost, all contribute to establishing the idea that everything is ephemeral. In "Self Portrait" the speaker laments: "Tiresome, tiresome is the poet / Recumbent on the davenport / Lost in raptures of self-regard / Give me poetry but pure [...] / I am what is wrong with America [...] / I am tired of all my yawn and barter. / How boring beauty is [...] Despite of my lovely diction / I am going to die" (95). Then suddenly, fifteen years later, there goes Sharon Stone, driving in her limousine, being beautiful and tiresome at the same time. So nothing changes but the dust, and the names we give it. There is thus a reduction at work in *Then Suddenly*—, which one does not find in *Hotel Fiesta,* as the instant moment of abstracting from the fact of dying and betrayal, which permeates *Hotel Fiesta* becomes a figurative representation in *Then Suddenly*—. Nothing escapes the symbolic world. Nothing but the moment when we forget to name our experiences, catalogue them by titling them.

The next chapter looks at what name poetry can assume, when it is made in the image of a more programmatic rather than radical concern with creative writing.

UNTITLED

Writer is pretty much tempted to quit writing.
—DAVID MARKSON

The thing one gradually comes to find out is that one has no identity that is when one is in the act of doing anything.
— GERTRUDE STEIN

Nowhere is the significance of proper names more culturally, literally, and aesthetically visible than in titles. A title in painting as well as written text is a paratext[1] that explores the relationship between the viewer or reader and the work under the title; the artist or writer and the title itself; and the artist or writer and influence. The specific title, "Untitled" – often encountered in connection with exhibited work at art museums – explores expectations of the unexpected and constitutes a movement towards searching. "Untitled" is a dynamic concept and reveals a kind of meta-consciousness about itself, insofar as it predicates all

---

1 See also Gerard Genette's influential book *Paratexts: Thresholds of Interpretation* (1987).

nominal functions. Although "title" and "untitled" cannot be juxtaposed, insofar as they do not share the same morphological level – "Title" is a noun, "Untitled" is an adjective – they do share some of the same paratextual functions. Whereas "Untitled" is an extremely common title that we encounter both in painting as well as literature, "Title" is something we have, not something we call "Title," which is to say that there are not many works whose title is "Title." "Title" uses its potential to name, define, describe, explain, represent, and interpret. "Untitled," on the other hand, is a paratext and a meta-paratext. "Untitled" is both a title and a title of a title. The difference between "title" and "untitled" is that the first is a fixation with the potential to engage expectation, while the latter is a movement towards the kind of expectation that is held down until something happens. In other words, "title" stands still, whereas "untitled" moves.

The act of titling, to title, involves the reader in a hermeneutics of desire: when we see a title we want to interpret it. Seeing the title, "Untitled," modifies our expectations which involves a hermeneutics of suspicion. Moreover, when we see the title of a work being "Untitled" we think of double agency. Is the work titled "Untitled" so titled by the author, or does it bear the name "Untitled" by default? "Untitled" thus seems to expropriate "Title" of its own primary function, which is to tell a story. Expropriation takes place when "Untitled" stands as a title to a work – and here I renounce the inverted commas around 'title' for generic purposes, thus indicating that "Untitled" is always a proper name, while title is a common noun. As in the earlier chapter on genius, here, I am also interested in expropriation, in the voluntary renunciation of property, rather than expropriation as a means of depriving of property.

While titles appropriate by taking images or themes from the work they ultimately name, and then accommodate these images to the language that ultimately forms the work at stake, "Untitled" undoes the act of appropriation by expropriating first the agent, and then the agent's property. Therefore expropriation refers to the state of "Untitled" in its meta-paratextual form. We can say that writers and artists expropriate themselves when they use "Untitled" as a title. In its original sense, expropriating oneself means voluntarily giving up one's property, that which belongs to oneself. Ultimately what one gives up is oneself.[2] However, "Untitled" by default is a second-hand act of expropriation. Curators or publishers name the works left untitled by artists "Untitled" for lack of a better term. Expropriation in this case happens at the point when the act of titling takes place in the gap, in *lieu* of, instead of another proper name.

One other distinction we can make in relation to the link between "Title" and "Untitled," which expropriation marks, is the difference between style and manner. Whereas we can talk about titles as a matter of style, when titles represent not just the form of the work but also its content, "Untitled" marks a manner of presentation that replaces the representation of form/content dichotomy with function. An example of title as style may be found in the message that links reading (the title) with expectation (not from the title but from the work): what you see is what you get (the reverse is, however, also possible). "Untitled" as

---

2 An example would be the predicament of women before the women's suffrage movement. If women had any property of their own, once entering marriage, it would all go to the husband, including the woman's 'self' – a notion which, at least where women's sense of selfhood is concerned, only came into full-fledged existence later with the counter-culture movement in the 60s.

manner offers a different relation: You cannot see the woods (work) for the trees (title) – therefore the work is left untitled. Thus words such as "title" and "untitled" conjure up a significant relation of difference between seeing and reading, writing and seeing. While "title" is more closely related to reading insofar as it has a narrative potential, the adjective "untitled," while nevertheless a title in its own right even though it is disguised or masked by its own paratext, calls for seeing beyond expectation. When reading a title one expects to see a certain symmetry between the title and the work that the title accompanies. Seeing a title such as "untitled" transforms reading (for we do read the letters) into a hermeneutics of desire. Whereas "title" marks a strategy of reading and seeing, "untitled" marks a poetics of the title's strategy by taking into account the act of writing. Unlike "title" whose function is to name and represent, "untitled" goes beyond naming to presenting writing to itself. "Untitled" is the manner of expropriating a title's style.

In her poem, "In Search of a Title" from *Then, Suddenly—*, Lynn Emanuel begins with a contemplation of an untitled work in the process not only of being created, but becoming a creation beyond description. The poem has four stanzas and it constitutes two moments of, first, "Untitled," represented in the first two stanzas, and second, "Title," represented in the last two stanzas. The speaker in the poem begins with a contemplation of the woods outside her porch where she sits, both staring at the trees and reading *The New York Book Review:*

> In *The Book Review* I read that nature is making
> a comeback which is one more thing to make me feel
> geeky and out-of-step. When's the literature
> of boarded-up shore towns coming back? As usual,

> I'm staring at the woods.
> (Emanuel, 1999: 50)

Towards the end of the second stanza the speaker realizes that she has been writing a poem for which she has no title. The need for titling grows out of the two first stanzas where the speaker's concern in the first one is with the text that she reads, while in the second stanza she is preoccupied with the object of reading from where she also seeks inspiration for her own work:

> Rachel Carson is saying, "If you understand nature,
> you will never be afraid or alone." So, I've set myself
> this small, unpleasant task: Describe the Tree as Though
> You Like It. (50)

The speaker shifts from contemplating the trees outside her house to reading about trees in her review. As the reading is interrupted by looking at the woods, the idea of taking the tree and describing it occurs to the speaker as a possibility for titling. Thus the title grows out of an "untitled" situation in which the tree, while not being represented, yet acts as a final possibility for a title. The tree is thus presented as a characteristic for the manner in which a description of the tree yields final results, here a title.

In the last two stanzas, where, again, we have a similar shift from text to object, the search for a title becomes more concrete and assumes self-conscious proportions as the speaker initiates a dialogue between writer, nature, and the nature of titling:

> a dogwood hovered above me, so thick and bright,
> it was as though the woods had spun a ghost; its pale
> and sloppily anthropomorphic form was more spacious
> and more flexible than "Tree." Humble and penetrating.

> Those are words that occur to me. Also, "dizzying
> freshet," but I reject that in favor of something less
> well-dressed. It's "spiffy" and "imprudent." The tree
> that is. That's why I like it. That white is a loose
>
> shirttail. Does it seem like bragging to say it reminds
> me of myself? I'd like to cast off Symbolisms – the need
> to stuff Thought and Feeling into the strongbox of Nature.
> What a giddy slosh of white ectoplasm the dogwood left
> on that blue sky. I'd like just to proceed, strolling along,
> side by side, as it were, immaculate, but unkempt. "White,"
> occurs to me. And "Naked." (51–52)

Although the speaker refers to *The Book Review* in the first stanza, a review that also works as an index for new titles on the market, she does not mention any titles as such. Thus the reference remains linked to a thematic account of a title, or several titles, dealing with a certain topic, here nature. Yet the representation of nature in the poem remains detached from its symbolism by the insertion of a momentary pause registered in the act of staring. "I'm staring at the woods," the speaker declares thus indicating a moment when nothing happens between thought and action, between thinking and writing. When staring, the gaze goes beyond the object in question to something imaginary yet related to the object that holds the viewer's fascination in check.

Thinking is held in suspension and constitutes the act of staring in its untitled mode. One can call this a moment of astonishment, one which, while not easily catalogued, awaits registration. It is as if some insight has just happened, but what it is obvious about it, escapes the poet. The more this escapes the poet, however, the more the poet is conscious of her writing poetry. The act of writing poetry thus takes place, but what it is precisely that the poet wants to say is not yet decided. Meanwhile, words become substance, they happen on the page, and there is hope, on the poet's part that she gets it right. This is one of the most crucial moments in poetry writing, namely the realization that one is on to something and that one will also get there before any articulation of a certain thought that calls "whatever" into being is turned into discourse that is not poetic, such as criticism, or philosophy may be.

More concretely, the speaker in this poem is obviously playing with the idiom: "I can't see the woods for the trees." One way of avoiding missing the woods is by titling it. Consequently, the speaker seems to suggest in the last two stanzas that perhaps "Tree" is not a good idea for a title if it is the woods one wants to see. Going from "Tree" to other words, which I also take as variations for titles such as "Humble and penetrating," and then to marking "spiffy" and "imprudent" as more likely candidates for titles as they are put in inverted commas, seems to suggest that the decision to title is linked to the desire to stylize the poem. The reason why the speaker ultimately renounces "Tree" as a title is precisely because it lacks style. As the wood takes on an anthropomorphic form suggesting a ghost-like cloud, the tree is seen in that relation as merely an object without the potential to represent. Thus, the desire is to keep searching for a title; the desire is to keep acting on behalf of staring at the wood and at the ghost, and thus make the untitled element in both expropriate the proper in the title. On a more general level, seeing the tree or the woods independently of each other suggests also a concern with background knowledge and specific knowledge. The first is something that one does not often have, but needs to have, while the second is a type that requires background if things are to be understood on a larger scale or for the purpose of seeing what their individuation consists of. Particularly in creative writing processes, the movement from the general to the specific is often enabled by a concern with either epistemic insight (background knowledge) or metaphysical insight (specific knowledge, which is yet abstract).

Pausing to consider the act of reading titles and reviewing them makes the speaker in the poem weary of the very task of titling. For titles function as witnesses to books' existence. An untitled work has no such witnesses, for which reason we can talk about a process of becoming that books and art alike engage in. Perhaps the idea of witnessing is what the speaker of the poem has in mind when references are made to the verticality of trees. In their vertical position trees remain in their potential state of becoming paper, they remain untitled works, whereas once down, trees are more likely to meet their (titular) fate in the form of books. Trees standing seem to assume agency and become themselves witnesses to changes in nature. Trees turned into paper, on the other hand, go back to being objects, yet witnessing this time the elaboration of writing, here in the form of titles. Regarding nature, a quick look at the results on searching for titles written by Rachel Carson, the well known scientist and environmental activist mentioned in the poem, discloses that there is at least one other book apart from Carson's own famous *Silent Spring* (1962) that bears a significant relation to the review that the speaker of the poem might be reading, namely *Witness for Nature* (1997), a biography of Carson's life written by environmental historian Linda J. Lear.

These speculations are prompted by Emanuel herself, insofar as the reader is invited to do her own searching for titles outside the poem. And yet, there is nothing outside the text, as Jacques Derrida famously proclaimed in his *Of Grammatology* (Derrida, 1974: 158), as our searching takes its point of departure not in reality but in fiction. We leave from the premise that the specific references in the poem to people and books correspond to a reality that we are in the position to identify. This reality is, however, represented as if in waiting to receive a title. Reality, then, is a representation of the untitled. Thus we are invited to consider the nature of the various concretizations of specific references that take place in the poem.

The speaker of Emanuel's poem herself concretizes issues such as writing, the nature of writing, the nature of nature, and the nature of any nature. The theme of nature is thus linked to the imagery of silence represented by the waiting for the return of the literature of "boarded-up shore towns." Together, nature and silence form the context of witnessing by staring, when 'nothing' happens. However, outside the (con)text of contemplation, something does happen, as a title, or else 'nothing' more than an "imprudent" feeling marks the arrival of a sense for a certain title. This sense is needed insofar as it is the only thing that begins the process of specification. One titles a work, or a thought, in order to make it specific.

In his paratextually playful essay, "Title (to be specified)," Jacques Derrida makes the following remark: "*the sense of the title is a certain manner of not having any and its event is one of not taking place*" (Derrida, 1981: 13; author's emphasis). Searching for titles is already a proleptic untitled act that mediates between the manner of not having any titles and the style of making 'nothing' specific. This much is clear from the way Emanuel's poem ends, with titles such as "White" and "Naked." Each of these titles stands for nature and nothing in their own way. While waiting for the literature of "boarded-up shore towns" (or rather paratexts in their own right) we are made to return to the blank of the white page and leave the event that does not take place naked.

Furthermore, in Emanuel's poem the theme of nature becomes a trope of imagery that puts an untitled mark on silence. Reading books and thinking about potential titles to title one's own books with is an activity that breaks nature's silent being. The observation that the speaker makes in the first line of the poem, "the woods are still here," coupled with the following question: "Can't the trees do something besides vertical?" is an attempt to recreate an ambiance in which the natural state of a tree takes on a symbolic quality as it moves into the normative social language as a title. The first title that comes to the speaker's mind is "Tree," but then it quickly gets dismissed insofar as "Tree" as a title does not fulfill the function of documentary representation.

Titles for Emanuel must operate as free agents. Therefore the representation of titles does not have an indexical quality. It has an expropriated quality. When, again, Giorgio Agamben asks "Why does poetry matter to us?" in his essay "Expropriated Manner," he probes the idea that the poet operates with free agency as she gives herself over to the unexpected (Agamben 1999b: 93). What is unexpected is the realization that manner, contrary to how the notion is generally perceived, as a twisted style, has in fact the same positive connotations as style. Agamben goes on to emphasize the importance of the medium of language that unites all opposing positions. Insofar as the poet "produces life" in the word, life produced in the poem "withdraws from both the lived experience of the psychosomatic individual and the biological unsayability of the species" (93). For Agamben expropriation links style to manner insofar as expropriation is seen as the experience of the poet who voluntarily gives up of herself. The manner in which the poet renounces her identity becomes the style that her poetry assumes.

Lynn Emanuel's registering of titles as names precisely at the point when the speaker wants to "cast off Symbolisms" parallels Agamben's insight for whom the poet's experience is an experience of style. As Emanuel appraises Thought's bias against the unanticipated, she seems to ask a similar question: Why do titles matter to us? When Agamben renders the notions of style and manner as two realities that correlate, he seems to suggest that in poetry the proliferation of titles must occur first through the prism of the untitled. Emanuel sees the poetic realm as the whiteness and nakedness of an aesthetics that perplexes every time a title is opposed consciously to the untitled. Says Agamben: "If style marks the artist's most characteristic trait, manner registers an inverse process of expropriation and exclusion. It is as if the old poet, who found his style and reached perfection in it, now forgets it in order to advance the singular claim of expressing himself solely through impropriety" (97).

Agamben's statement brings to mind the work of a symbolist, Henri Michaux and his relation to the expropriation of manner that is similar to the process of searching for titles by positing them in an improper relation to the untitled. Michaux asks a question in the same manner that Emanuel does when her speaker sits on the porch anticipating the literature that would take the form of the titles 'in stare,' as it were: "Could it be that I draw because I see so clearly this thing or that thing? Not at all. Quite the contrary. I do it to be perplexed again. And I am delighted that there are traps. I look for surprises" (Michaux, 1963). The interesting thing about work dealing with the expropriation of manner in one way or another is that it tends to appear under titles bearing such titles as "Untitled." In a way, one can contend that both states of being either astonished or perplexed are untitled states to begin with. They are just there, as they happen, and mark a world as it is independent of what it is named, precisely as this world suggests things in it that are already there whether discovered or not. Perplexity and astonishment, then, belong to a thing-in-itself world, *an sich*. This world is ideally understood by the poet as it gives itself over to the poet's discovery through a mental process that relies on making compatible one's background knowledge of the world with its specificity.

In Michaux's work, which can be likened to Emanuel's where the metaphorical understanding of knowledge as background or specific is concerned, that which is not known is not refuted, but made passages for, which may lead to an understanding of a unified formulation of what to call what we see. Michaux's work has also been published under the title *Untitled Passages* which combines a number of his untitled drawings with poems from the volume *Passages* (De Zegher, 2000). Michaux's research into the passages between "title" and "untitled" can be said to function as a search into the passages between writing and seeing. For Michaux writing is seen as an expression of the improper in drawing, and the consequence of such an expropriation of the proper particularly and conversely in writing has had a strong influence in the work of John Ashbery, who not only translated Michaux but also let Michaux's "untitles" find way into his own poetry. Ashbery himself wrote a prose poem called "Untilted" (Ashbery,

1981) – and it is not a spelling mistake! – in which he probes the limitations of language by alluding to the symbolist desire to merge drama and fiction, writing and seeing by designating passages for the expression of the improper manner in a proper style appropriated precisely by and through expropriation. Ashbery's "Untilted" that at first glance one always reads as "Untitled," plays on the visual closeness between tilting and titling. Ashbery thus performs a similar movement of expropriation by leading his poem into a state of proper nonidentity.

Michaux was not just a painter but also a writer of prose poems concerned with the works of symbolism through the movements of darkness. If for symbolists such as Michaux, language and consciousness, taken as one item, is about expropriating the proper manner of seeing, language and consciousness has a different expropriating manner for poets such as Emanuel who introduces writing itself as the element that moves darkness not in the realm of whiteness or seeing, but in the realm of nakedness or reading. I recall here a statement I made at the beginning of this chapter: "Untitled moves" for the sake of creating a parallel with what one may see as the gist of symbolism: darkness moves.

The reason why Emanuel's speaker wants to cast off symbolisms is due to the poet's experience and her ability to produce life in words, name life and give it titles. Emanuel's title, "Naked," at the end of her poem is a title that expropriates precisely the manner in which the poet moves through darkness. On the other hand, the two titles that occur to the speaker towards the end of the poem, namely, "White" and "Naked," emphasize the blank page as an event in waiting for something to happen as it happens. What happens in this case is the untitled title. "White" and "Naked," in other words, are clear examples of titles for the "Untitled." Therefore "title" and untitled" can be said to stand in a reciprocal relation to one another, with title becoming some sort of an archive containing the untitled. The title is the style of the untitled manner. Says Agamben:

> Only in their reciprocal relation do style and manner acquire their true sense beyond the proper and the improper. The free gesture of the writer lives in the tension between these two poles: style is an *expropriating appropriation*, a sublime negligence, a self-forgetting in the proper; manner is an *appropriating expropriation*, a presentiment or resemblance of oneself in the improper. Not only in the old poet but in every great writer (Shakespeare!) there is a manner that distances itself from style, a style that expropriates itself into manner. At its height, writing even consists in precisely the interval – or, rather, the passage – between the two. Perhaps in every field but most of all in language, use is a polar gesture: on the one hand, appropriation and habit; on the other, expropriation and nonidentity. And "usage" (in its whole semantic field, as both "to use" and "to be used to") is the perpetual oscillation between a homeland and an exile – dwelling. (Agamben, 1999b: 98)

For Emanuel, Agamben's presentiment as resemblance finds resonance in the identification of titles with the poet. Yet another question that the speaker poses: "That white is a loose shirttail. Does it seem like bragging to say it reminds me of myself?" constitutes a passage à la Michaux's *Untitled Passages* that correlates and corresponds to the idea of dwelling. Titles stand still, I recall yet another line from the beginning of this chapter, in the same manner that we can say titles dwell, while untitled manners pass in the same way that we can say untitled passages move.

Thus for Lynn Emanuel the expropriation of titles is not only contingent on the process of untitling but also on intertextuality in the sense that the search for a title becomes a movement towards comprehending not how the writer chooses the titles but how the titles choose the writer. Registering and making an archive for the titles rendered in the poem is a reinforcement of the intertexts that make Emanuel's poems prose poems of becoming.

Such intertexts come to the fore in *Then, Suddenly*— through the use of other paratexts, not just titles but also epigraphs. Three epigraphs each standing before one of the three divisions in the book play not on the subjectivization of language but on the subjectivization of becoming. "I," "it," and "you" are the untitled forms of the title "Naked." The epigraph from Calvino for the book's Part 1, with an emphasis on the "I" and the "you": "I am called 'I' and this is the only thing you know about me, but this alone is reason enough for you to invest a part of yourself in the stranger 'I'" (5), appraises the unanticipated "it," which is the drive of the performative movement expressed in the Einstein epigraph to Part 2: "Nothing happens until something moves" (25). The third epigraph from Gertrude Stein to Part 3 in which we find the poem "In Search of a Title" brings "title" and "untitled" in a reciprocal relation to narration: "Think of narrative from this thing, a narrative can give emotion because an emotion is dependent upon a succession upon a thing having a beginning and a middle and an end" (45).

The overall search for titles in *Then, Suddenly*— culminates anaphorically in the master epigraph from Edmond Jabès that begins the entire collection, the entire book: "The book is the subject of the book." Here Emanuel exorcises symbolisms out of the shifting passages between "title" and "untitled." This is suggested already, and in a most ingenious way, in the very first poem, one which is situated between the Jabès quote and the Calvino epigraph. This poem, also tellingly titled, "Like God," stands all by itself, alone, between text and paratext. And the fact that its title, as it is marked by punctuation, by a comma, indicates some sort of action, furthermore demonstrates that the very notion of 'then suddenly' can be performed any time, every time, but not so much as an anticipation of a future but more as its assurance. The search for a title constitutes a poem of becoming insofar as it questions the relationship between the realization of self-consciousness and its actualization in estrangement. Thus "In Search of a Title" discloses an instance of "expropriated" mannerism that manifests an "improper" relation of being to becoming.

In this poem not only does the writer expropriate the manner in which God creates, but also appropriates his style albeit differently: the male God with a white beard is here represented as a woman who has been anticipating her own arrival, her own *becoming* a writer: "You have been expecting yourself / as a woman who purrs by in a dress by Patou" (3), we are told. Then the writer also expropriates the manner in which she herself creates, as God did, by appropriating the reader's power to understand what writing is all about. It is thus the reader who ultimately *is* like God, who makes choices for her reading strategies and who chooses the story in which she wants to appear, in which she just *is*:

> ...although you knew all along
> the road would be there, you, who have
> been hovering above this page, holding
> the book in your hands, like God, reading. (4)

The title *is*. The untitled *becomes*.

PORTRAIT

> *Refinanced memory*
> *washes white.*
> —ROSMARIE WALDROP

> *Certainly some who were certain that this one was a great man*
> *and one clearly expressing something*
> *and greatly expressing something being struggling*
> *were listening to this one telling about being living*
> *telling about this again and again and again.*
> —GERTRUDE STEIN

Reconstructing notions such as potentiality and inspiration, Emanuel's prose poems, whose thematic range spans from involvement with the paintings of Emanuel's renowned father, Akiba Emanuel, (a model and 'pupil' of Matisse), to the 'portraits' of Gertrude Stein, illuminate the interrelationship between language and world, and the psychology of inhabiting both through inspiration. This chapter addresses the question of what fuels creativity when it is put to work through the involvement of other voices that are represented (in Emanuel's case) as suffering from having their genius interrupted either by death, by lack of recognition, or by amnesia. In all Emanuel's collections of poems, including her chap-books as well, inspiration plays an important role. Yet Emanuel is not interested in inspiration in the traditional sense to mean divine connection with a higher power or a muse, and romantic transcendence. Inspiration for Emanuel is always triggered by an attempt at understanding what pain is. The pain of creation and composition together with the pain of reading and writing promote two different types of understanding: first, that there is something to create out of nothing, and second, that 'nothing' is always a beginning. Inspiration for Emanuel is therefore the beginning of nothing. But how does one begin nothing, a created nothing, that is, a nothing that can be rendered and read, one that can explain both the pain of understanding such relations and the inspiration that befalls them? One of Emanuel's answers seems to be given through her use of amnesia. It is through the theme of forgetfulness that a connection between the writer and the reader is established.

Emanuel is particularly a poet who writes for an audience for whom poetry means the objectification of subjects. In spite of her attempt at going beyond the poetics of modernism and its concern with inspiration as a relationship between the act of writing and death, she is close to some of the questions that concerned writers such as James Joyce. Joyce's question in *Ulysses*: "What idiosyncrasies of the narrator were concomitant products of amnesia? (Joyce, 1992: 854) can be traced in some of Emanuel's poems that research the ground covered by forgetfulness. For Emanuel, how to construe a narrative out of nothing, how to objectify the nothing and then tell a story about it is an endeavor that involves the creative minds of others.

Emanuel, like her father before her, draws inspiration from the human figure as it is capable of experience. In an interview she recalls her father's imperatives when she grew up in an environment where art meant the practice of either painting or poetry writing: "Lynn, draw that vase, make it your mother. Turn the green curtain into the woods she's walking into" (Domangue, 1997: http). Emanuel's father, whose paintings only now are getting their deserved recognition and attention, was a master especially in the portraiture genre. Interestingly enough, however, some of his still life paintings can also pass as portraits especially insofar as they exhibit a human allure that calls for a very specific response to them, namely they are very painful to look at. According to Avis Berman, who wrote an essay accompanying a major exhibition of Akiba Emanuel's work at the Alexander Gallery in New York, Emanuel's art "was not a career, or a vocation, but a way to resolve his most private and intense emotional stresses and conundrums, which is why he willfully challenges viewers to recognize and comprehend him only if they dare" (Berman, 1993: no pagination).

Daring to confront Akiba Emanuel is a challenge mostly poets are invited to take up insofar as they share in the creative process a concern with interiority. As Berman puts it: "Akiba was a creator of interiors, psychological and actual," which enforces Akiba Emanuel's own statement regarding the predicament of the artist: "there are no short cuts, creation is difficult, requiring every fiber of your mind and soul. It is an enormous personal sacrifice, there is no rest from it" (no pagination). The implication of Akiba Emanuel's credo is that the artist can only create if he forgets himself. His art can only be worth looking at if it encompasses this forgetfulness.

It is against such a background that Lynn Emanuel's own voice emerges. Poems such as "Inspiration" and "Inspiration, Two" from *The Dig* function as portraits of the human experience as it is traceable in the poem-portrait itself. Writes Emanuel in "Inspiration":

> I am tired of the tundra of the mind,
> where a few shabby thoughts hunker
> around a shabby fire. All day from my window
> I watch girls and boys hanging out
> in the dark arcades of adolescent desire.
>
> Tonight, everything is strict with cold,
> the houses closed, the ice botched by skaters.
> I am tired of saying things about the world,
> and yet, sometimes, these streets are so
> slick and bold they remind me of the wet
>
> zink bar at the Café Marseilles, and suddenly the sea
> is green and lust is everywhere in a red cravat,
> leaning on his walking stick and whispering,
> I am a city, you are my pilgrim,
> meet me this evening. Love, Pierre.
> (Emanuel, 1995: 42)

This poem's double take on inspiration, first as a paratext in the title and then as a theme that informs the title as well, is an attempt at forging together the experience of having had a lover, desiring to forget him, and the pain in responding by rushing to meet the lover when he calls. The sense of weariness and tiredness of things previously said is also a sense that is conducive to inspiration that is guided by pain and amnesia. The speaker's declarations of fatigue are in fact performances of an amnesiac psychology of the pain experienced, that is, the pain of wanting to forget how events turn into non-events. In his "Amnesis Manifesto" the Bolivian poet and literary critic Nicomedes Suárez-Araúz argues that "the totality of human existence is circumscribed by amnesia" and that "amnesia is everything and nothing, qualities which have been attributed to divinities" further suggesting that, insofar as amnesia is also a source of inspiration, it is certain. Its certainty affirms what Suárez-Araúz claims is the "undeniable presence and essence of our personal and collective worlds" (Suárez-Araúz, 1984: http).

By the same token the speaker or narrator in Emanuel's poem is not inspired by what she remembers she has forgotten but by the certainty with which she asserts her forgotten experience of having been certain places and having seen certain things. It is the amnesiac inspiration that brings about the sudden change in the colors of the sea and Pierre's cravat, which in the quoted lines is imagined but later in the last stanza materialized as such. What Emanuel is interested in portraying in this poem is how the distance between the speaker and the listener is obliterated by the various idiosyncrasies in the experience of pain.

The poem "Inspiration, Two" follows a timeline that seemingly obliterates what Joyce calls "the migrations in narrator and listener" to the point where what is given is, in Joyce's apt words, "the consequence of the action of distraction upon vicarious experiences" (Joyce, 1992: 854). While amnesia seems to be a notion that seems to know itself in spite of us and our obliviousness, it also marks an unknown time that we nonetheless experience. What interests me in these poems is the relationship between experience and amnesia as a manifestation of pain and inspiration. When Emanuel writes in "Inspiration, Two" that "the problem is how to say / smartly what is used to being said beautifully, only" (Emanuel, 1995: 57) she returns to the idea of depicting, rather in pictorial terms, the colors of pain, and the inspiration inherent in oblivion.

There is a subtle hint here to the languages that a poet and a painter speak. A poet seeks to be smart, whereas as a painter seeks beauty. Growing up in places other than where she was born, namely Denver, Colorado, Emanuel is preoccupied with the loss of action and occurrences that such places as New York are capable of. The fact that nothing ever happens in places such as Denver, in Emanuel's depiction, "the featureless amnesias of Idaho, Nebraska, Nevada, / states rich only in vowel sounds and alliteration" (Emanuel, 1999: 7) causes the speaker of the poem "Out of Metropolis" to seek to solve the tension between action and beauty, between occurrence and forgetfulness. The underlying question here seems to be, to what extent does inspiration matter when the mediation of one's position vis-à-vis one's dwelling place is filtered through amnesia?

From poems that depict inspiration in an objectified form Emanuel has moved into the realm where the figure of the father becomes an inspiration, yet separate from the way in which the loss of a creative mind is being dealt with. Emanuel's *Then, Suddenly—* begins with the quick energy of movement, then slows down, and moves more contemplatively towards new beginnings that seem to have life at a standstill. From depicting portraits of places, much in the same manner as her father depicted objects with a human soul, Emanuel engages in a process of depicting and dealing with the pain of losing her father. As Andrena Zawinski remarks in her review of *Then, Suddenly—*, Emanuel's deceased father "interrupts the text, its narrative, its poetry, much like anyone might be interrupted by the voice of grief when it seems to speak to us" (Zawinski, http). Here I would suggest that while the interruption of narrative comes from a desire to forget the painful event, it also functions as the initiator for a sought after moment of inspiration.

In the poem "Halfway Through the Book I'm Writing," which announces already in the title that the role of the reader is not just to read but watch how the event of portrayal takes place, Emanuel's speaker takes over the voice of the dead father and a certain psychology of inspiration is triggered. The event of pain is turned into a plot, the result being a portrayal of a character who partakes in the action of writing poetry. As Emanuel puts it:

> My father dies and is buried in his Brooks Brothers suit.
> But I can't seem to keep him underground.
> Suddenly, I turn around and there he is just
> as I'm getting a handle on the train-pulls-
>
> into-the-station poem. "What gives?"
> I ask him. "I'm alone and dead," he says,
> and I say, "Father, there's nothing I can do about
> all that. Get your mind off it. Help me with the poem
>
> about the train. "I hate the poem about the train,"
> he says. But since he's dead and I'm a patient woman
> I turn back to the poem in which the crowds have gone home
> and the janitor pushes the big mustache of his broom
> across the floor,
> and I ask, "Dad, is that you in there?"
>
> "No it's not." (Emanuel, 1999: 27)

Emanuel's exteriorization of a need to get help in the creative act of writing a poem, as she had forgotten what she wanted to write, is an expression of how collective memory works. In her case here, it works by proxy. The question "What gives?" can be understood as an attempt to avoid backtracking into myth and history, as that would mean a search for amnesiacs who cannot recognize each other. In Emanuel's poem the father becomes a cloud resembling Magritte's bowler who hangs over the train station giving instructions as to what her poem should contain, further demanding:

> "I want to go to a museum; put one in the poem
> beside the station."
> [...] "And when I get to the museum I want to see
> Soutine, Miró, Picasso, or Dali, I want eyes in my armpits
> And my fingers, eyes in the air, the trees, the dirt." (28)

What the speaker has to say about the father's discourse is the remark that he is already "an eye-in-the-dirt." The idea that the father is able to express desires beyond the grave in a visual way by literally turning his fragmented self into the object of seeing, the eye-in-the-dirt, is interesting on two accounts: first, because it points to the relation between decomposition and composition and second because it formulates an aesthetics of inspiration. Akiba Emanuel, who himself has gone through a cubist period, seems here to suggest that only by going to the museum and being reminded of others' works of art can one, say, forget about Picasso, or Miró, and catch your own train. Thus, what is emphasized here is the fact that oblivion marks a division between a poet and her precursor and functions as the condition for the representation of an interior — be it the grave, or the psyche. Only in this divide can one go beyond immediate self-expression and instead of merely representing, perform a creative act. In his book, *The Theory of Inspiration,* Timothy Clark forwards the claim, similar to Akiba Emanuel's idea of interiority, that a writer's conception of a creative inner power is often "an image of an anticipated rhetorical effect" (Clark, 1997: 10). Writes Clark:

> The aesthetic of inspiration has not always been the simplistic notion of heightened and immediate self-expression for which it is now usually taken. Instead, it often situates the act of composition as a space of division, rupture or possibility between the mundane subjectivity of the writer and alternative and usually unforeseeable modes of being or subjectivity to which the unique interaction and intercontamination of the psychic and textual seems to give access. Inspiration recurrently forms part of an anti-formalist aesthetic which renders composition a kind of experiment upon the writer's psyche and received determinations both of the human and of art. (119)

The father's decomposition in Emanuel's poem, his imperative to forget about writing poems and go to museums instead, is a way of defamiliarizing the traditional notion of inspiration. The artist's pain and anxiety of influence, to use Harold Bloom's idea, is here dealt with by transforming the anticipated rhetorical effect of the working of imagination, the rhetoric of interiority that is, not into composition but decomposition.

In her other poems from the same collection dealing with the figure of the father, Emanuel anchors the notion of decomposed inspiration to a poetics of self-empowerment following the construction of pain as a death-drive. Writes Emanuel in "The Burial":

> After I've goosed up the fire in the stove with *Starter Logg*
> so that it burns like fire on amphetamines; after it's imprisoned,
> screaming and thrashing, behind the stove door; after I've
> listened to the dead composers and watched the brown-
> plus-gray deer compose into Cubism the trees whose
> name I don't know (pine I think); after I've holed up in my
> loneliness staring at the young buck whose two new antlers
> are like a snail's stalked eyes and I've let this conceit lead me
> to the eyes-on-stems of the faces of Picasso and from there
> to my dead father; after I've chased the deer away […];
> then I bend down over the sea of keys to write this poem
> about my father in his grave.
>
> It isn't easy.
> (Emanuel, 1999: 29)

Standing by the father's grave with a shovel in her hand the speaker goes on to notice the inert body of her father drooping besides her as if in a state of anesthesia. The interesting thing about anesthesia is that it induces the body in a state of unconsciousness with the absence of pain sensation, in other words, it blocks the memory so that the body becomes either catatonic or amnesiac. In Emanuel's poem there is a desire to undo the inevitable pain by identifying parts of the speaker's body with the objects surrounding her, here particularly the shovel. The speaker's arm becomes an extension of the shovel. As she puts it, "it grows cool and sedate under the influence of his flesh," thus suggesting that the memory of what one is doing, taking an active part in burying another, can be obliterated by making the body enter a state of sedation. There is thus a tension between action and inertia that is felt not only throughout this poem, but also throughout the whole book. Being under the influence of the decomposed body is what enables the speaker to compose herself both literally and metaphorically. The last line of the poem thus reads: "The body alone, in the dark, in the cold, without a coat. I would not wish that on my greatest enemy. Which, in a sense, my father was" (30).

Then, Suddenly— begins, as the title itself indicates, with a double aim: to anticipate and then render the plot of a story. The second part of the book, although having action as slow motion, is very much concerned with how quickly we perceive occurrences. The thematization of trains and transportation in the first part acquires a metaphorical significance, akin to the situation when we say that some news hits us like a train.

As mentioned in the previous chapter, the book's second part is furthermore accompanied by an epigraph by Einstein that makes us think of Einstein's thought experiments with trains, which are now famous. The epigraph reads: "Nothing happens until something moves" (25). Einstein's statement is here part of the poet's general formulation of a poetics of inspiration that exalts the resources of amnesia, yet not at the expense of action, but by making forgetfulness an action with potential. This much is expressed in the poems that deal with self-portraiture. Having pushed for movement forward and by empowering herself with death beyond the grave, the speaker of the poem "Persona" informs us:

> When the reader's radar tracked me down,
> I had given up and become the dead man.
> I throbbed in the big fog of his white shirt.
> I called down the long tunnel of his throat
> *Oh dead man, where are we going?* He called back —
> *Everybody is a door: Open: Enter: Become:* (34)

Taking over the body of a man, impersonating him by wearing his coat, the speaker inhabits the dead man's subjectivity. Interestingly, however, this is not done without first making recourse to the numbing of the senses, here in the form of lobotomy, which is also a component of amnesia. As the speaker puts it:

> [...] I shoved my head
> into the mouth of his tragic hat, I donned
> the trench coat with the lobotomy, and just like
> that, I was a man. On my finger I bore the tourniquet
> of his ring, and I was happy inside my lonely
> rayon blazer when a voice said suddenly –
>
> LYNN EMANUEL, IS THAT YOU IN THERE?
>
> *No,* I said, standing there clothed in the raiment
> of a dead man. *No,* said the voice of the dead
> man limping up and down the stairs of my voice.
> *No, no, no,* said the voice of the dead man limping
> down the long dark corridor of my throat. (34)

Forgetfulness here functions as the door opened towards the potential to become another person, especially a dead person. The speaker who does not want to identify herself as Lynn Emanuel wants the reader to forget about the author and relate her reading experience not to the senses in the poem but its plot and its anticipated action as suggested also by the colon following the italicized word *Become.*

It can be contended that Emanuel's poems in their advocating for a relation between the writer and the reader, in which each forgets the other, yet each is given the possibility to contemplate the functionality of reading and writing, are poems that engage with inspiration in a decomposed way. That is to say, Emanuel's poems are consolidations of the absent, circular, and amnesiac nature of inspiration. One is inspired but only in a fictional, decomposed way.

In his introduction to the collection of short stories and excerpts from novels dealing with amnesia, titled *The Vintage Book of Amnesia*, Jonathan Lethem makes the following observation on what characterizes the protagonist suffering from amnesia: "an even more disheartening realization for the amnesiac is that he's *only a fictional character.* Call it Pirandello's Syndrome" (Lethem, 2000: xv). Emanuel's poems seem to have the same quality to them: they are impersonations of a fictional character who forgets she is the author and as such is in search for a reader who would deliver her from the forgotten memory of a pain that is portrayed as potent inspiration. Emanuel's poems are inspirations of a forgotten genre, one which has "the book as the subject of the book," to quote the Edmond Jabès epigraph for the whole of *Then Suddenly—*. What remains to be considered, after things happen, after they happen suddenly, after they have been named, and then pulverized, is the ensuing pause following a contemplative moment of what one has done, or witnessed, or expressed in writing or in painting. The dash. The hegemony of absence.

If one considers Emanuel's earlier work in *The Dig*, one notices how the relation between the present and the past is articulated in a less tensioned and problematic way than in *Then Suddenly—*. The dominant feeling in *The Dig*, for instance, is that after a whole lot of digging for relics from the past, what is archived in memory, or stored in rooms is just the usual business marked by a certain pragmatic urgency: you want to discover something, you discover it, on with the story. The sections that make up *The Dig* also suggest this efficiency in the compartmentalization of feelings and events through titles that indicate where we are in the story line. "The Beginning, Beginning Again, Past and Present, The Hearafter and After That, Coda (in the form of notes)." What one finds at and between these stages may be the result of sudden discovery, but the sudden moment as such is never pressing, nor impinging on the ensuing events. The feeling that something ominous is about to happen is not something that the speaker in these poems wants to dwell too much on. Quite the contrary. If a situation is identified as grave, it is also shown instantly that it is the human folly that made it so, and hence not so serious after all, but rather something that we can all laugh at in the end.

It can be said that while these poems deal with 'the instant,' in *Then Suddenly*— it is 'the sudden' that is the problem. In *The Dig*, the poem "We, the Poets of America," [and then in the first line] don't have time for Istanbul" (40) emphasizes the same demand for instant resolution that one also finds in lines that are examples of yet another instance of notional *ekphrasis*, this time in photography. The going from the present to the past is also a going from the collective body that makes up a family or a nation to the individual. We, the poets of America, who don't have time for history, also used to be a more romantic individual poet caught in time at a certain age, and looking a certain way. In the poem "Self-Portrait at Eighteen" the speaker, after nostalgically having been through a box of photographs, ends with these lines:

> Still, I love the delicate bones of my pelvis (the bony repose that suggests, as well, the sculptures on sarcophagi) in this photograph which a not-quite-forgotten-enough-photographer entitled: *Portrait of a Woman, Nude*. (Emanuel, 1995: 39)

Things are uncanny, statuesque, and cold as marble, but still. Such getting-over-with things, or feelings, is also suggested in another poem from *The Dig* that can be seen as a parallel to "The Burial" in *Then Suddenly*—. "What Grieving Was" in *The Dig* is precisely an instant of wonder, caught and fixated under the wheels of a hearse. The speaker, here a small girl attending a funeral, expresses her astonishment over death as it relates to observing objects as they appear in time rather than the way in which she perceives them in an almost out of the body experience, which is the case in "The Burial." Thus we read the concluding lines, which can also be said to perform precisely the statement, "what grieving was:"

> The grandfather clock's pendant
> An unaffordable gold told the quarter hour.
>
> The hearse rolled forward over the *O*'s
> Of its own surprise. (27)

In terms of structural composition *The Dig* links the thematic of the book – which is delivered as a form of an imperative: 'dig beyond the surface' – with shifts in style that enforce the theme of 'the instant'. Up until the coda at the end of the volume, what we are presented with are poems in a more traditional form. "The Coda (in the form of notes)," however, marks a shift to something else. As it announces its own internal structure in its title, it reads almost as a fragmentary diary that insists on the instance of the poet's death. The Coda re-features the sections in the book and thus succeeds in depicting a very concise portrait of the writer who, if in mourning, then, is in mourning over her own death. Thus we read in the fragment, *The Beginning*:

> And now you see me. I am sitting, typing by the window, a thin woman in a flowered housedress. Perhaps you wonder who I am. I am the voice-over. I am the writer. My hand is on the rattle of the bomb. And this is my story. I was poor. I wrote. I killed myself. (70)

After a chronological following of events, such as the speaker's moving to Ely with her mother, and then going abroad, in the fragment *Past and Present,* Rome's decaying beauty becomes the site of an awakening. The speaker snaps out of her lethargy, and makes concrete her experience of life, particularly as a life deeply entangled with an acute awareness of the power of words. Thus we, and a personified Rome, are told:

> "Bella Roma": My poetry, as you can see, has been repeatedly diminished and deformed by the actual. Every moment of transcendence plummets to an anxious consideration of the economic terms of my life: food, shelter, and so on. So, too, do all these poems hint at a thematic concern I've dealt with more directly elsewhere: I have been highly involved in "the romance of not being listened to." This accounts for the sense of the soliloquist in much of my work. At times, I may have achieved a peculiar originality because one premise of my writing is this: I have had total liberty because I have had total anonymity. As I wrote in letter to a friend, "All my life it has been as though I am already dead." (72)

Who can argue with the instance of the poet's death, especially as it is always depicted in conditional terms? While *The Dig* clearly operates with full-stops, insofar as they are mediated by a conditional state, they thus open for the dash, always following the instant of 'then suddenly,' not as a temporal relation but as an event.

HEGEMONY

Give voice to the voiceless.
Think about the word "give" and what you are claiming, who you are in speaking;
can you "give" and what work does this rhetorical word really accomplish?
—RACHEL BLAU DUPLESSIS

Grammar is pronounced.
—GERTRUDE STEIN

Prior to her now complete manuscript awaiting publication, *Noose and Hook* (2010), one that I shall discuss more amply in the last chapter of this book, Lynn Emanuel shared with me some poems that led to her developing more fully her concern with the political situation in the US and its consequences for aesthetic production. These poems are particularly interesting insofar as they display a new linguistic idiom that shows, almost performatively, a process through which American ideals can be said to be pulverized under the weight of hegemony. On my part, I am particularly attracted to the idea of engaging with writing about pulverizations against the background of 'non-official' texts, as it were. The writing is there, to be sure, and I have license from

Emanuel to write about this as yet unpublished material, but I find it challenging to look at the poems from a compositional point of view, which is to say that I am interested in following closely into the footsteps of a creative process that has the destabilization of hegemonic acts as a double aim: first, thematically through the search for or through the invention of a new idiom or formal language that expresses the extent to which resistance is possible, and then by performatively moving towards expressing what resistance can consist of, what function it has, and what consequences it carries for the subject who identifies with lower species, in this case here with barking dogs. Thus I begin with what initially was a draft, yet I shall juxtapose in the relevant places the text of what later became a 'final' poem in *Noose and Hook*. This chapter should consequently be regarded as a transanalysis of a text in transit, but one which has the potential to enrich the understanding of Emanuel's new work insofar as it considers the poet's trajectory of thought as it struggles to depart from conventional frameworks of perception.

Drawing on influences by John Berryman's *Dream Songs* and George Herriman, a famous cartoonist whose drawings and language were based on the English spoken by immigrants – with German, Italian, and Yiddish accents – Emanuel's intent is to assess to what extent "the US hast gone to the dogs."[1] Making recourse to the voice of an unnamed dog narrator, she investigates the consequences of poverty and class distinction for various communities of people who are always off beat, yet relentless in

---

[1] I am grateful to Lynn Emanuel for letting me know about these two sources of inspiration in the writing of these poems. In the final work of *Noose and Hook* both Berryman and Herriman are acknowledged, the latter also in the form of a poem dedicated directly to him.

their dealings with authority figures. Transferring the focus from the actions of policing dogs to the action of observant dogs – Herriman's Ofissa Pupp is a police(man)dog always out to put Ignatz, the arrogant mouse, in jail for his not reciprocating Krazy Kat's romantic feelings for him – Emanuel's poems, with their emphasis on barking, have the effect of swishing and hurling a dagger at dogs that merely wag their tails and tongues without swaying anybody.

Following composition and content closely I want to look here not only at how portraits of dogs reveal the state of the art where current American affairs are concerned on several levels, but also at the way in which Emanuel's dog-language, while constituting an eloquent critique of the US, also lends itself to an aesthetic of choice and potentiality. The guiding questions that she seems to ask here are: to what extent we can have non-humans speak for us, and if that is the case, then, what would be the consequences of our choosing to listen to, and therefore abide by the laws of a potentially new type of hegemony? Insofar as Emanuel renders the notion of community in a potential state, yet whose structure is actualized in the sense that the beings in the dog community share the same space but are not together in any communal sense, I find her idea that there are doors at which one can keep barking persuasive. I see the dog's implicit 'open sesame' barking as a way of engaging with hegemony both in its domestic as well as potential states. One of the finalized poems in *Noose and Hook,* and whose title is "Dogg's House" emphasizes the tension between *fait-accompli* acts, unknown powers, resoluteness, and a continuous sense of expectation. The first line reads: "They tolt me each dogg has its door. / i wakt up to this one" (25).

Insofar as the members of a community identify with the ideas that hegemony passes off as commonsensical, hegemony can be said to have a domestic form, at least where the community's sense of belonging is concerned. However, the domestic aspect of hegemony is also challenged whenever the community has to deal with differences across class, gender, race (and species). While there are no alternatives to hegemony, what makes power less stable, and therefore more of a potential than an actualization is the idea of difference. Here I am particularly interested in tracing different types of hegemonic manifestations as they encompass the type of community that does not merely designate shared space but is also very much what has been excluded from it; in other words, it is also constituted by that lack.

Emanuel's quite developed community in terms of self-awareness perceives hegemony not only by pointing to the implications of class, codes, and images, but also by looking at hegemony in its potential state. If we return briefly to Agamben's insights, we notice that, for the philosopher, the idea of a community beyond essence is realized only as a kind of potential belonging, or a linguistic belonging *par excellence.* By shifting the linguistic codes from signification to potentiality, Emanuel, much in the same vein as Agamben would have it, suggests that communities are an effect of the hegemonic subject/object relation but only insofar as this relation is part of *impotentiality* or that which is also a necessary and an integral part of the kind of potentiality that opens a space for sharing and not sharing at the same time.

Emanuel's cycle of dog poems, which in its draft form was called *Dogge Songs* (2006), of which I have a sample that consists of three poems, commences with a prologue in which the question: "Where duz my song open?" is followed by a paragraph that sets the tone of the poems and reads almost like a stage direction:

> The seam opens along a beach and a leadin sky and in the distance a modest heap of modest nothin but lots of empty parkin lots uf gulls r blank white pages scattered thither and further off there is sum war, sum ships and trains, sum chips and stains. (Emanuel, 2006)

The diction in these poems is modified and follows the tone and style of medieval English. The three epigraphs[2] that accompany the prologue reveal Emanuel's interest in conceptual form. The language that Emanuel lets her dogs speak comes out of trying out archaic typographies and seeing how they feel, sound, and ultimately build a community. The first epigraph from the Middle English writer William Langland's *Piers Plowman* (1330-1387) reads: *Thi dogge dar nat berke,* and is followed by a second epigraph from John Berryman: —— *You is from hunger, Mr. Bones.* This is a line from Berryman's *Dream Songs* (1964), which is a book composed of 77 poems revolving around the character Henry, his life and tribulations, and witty conversations with an unnamed narrator. For the most part Berryman's protagonist not only goes by the name of Mr. Bones, a dog name, but also behaves like a dog. Berryman's poems are celebrated for their play with language, particularly the inventive syntax and the renunciation to creating complete utterances. The first two epigraphs, while giving us an indication of the play and tension between archaisms and neologisms are also masking the hegemony inher-

---

2 In the final work, *Noose and Hook*, all the epigraphs mentioned here have been dropped. Their influence is, however, felt on several levels, which will be pointed out in the last chapter.

ent in language as they are followed by a descriptive line in the third epigraph attributed to the OED: *One paire of dogges sits in the Chymley.* Now, insofar as chimneys were a reflection of grievance, as houses were taxed all according to how many they had (Bush, 1991), Emanuel's reference and use of the old spelling alerts the reader that the poems are as much about the consequence of current tax laws in the US as they are about allegorical dream visions in which dogs become spokesmen for an active poetic expression which, by its nature, cannot be abolished. The songs are thus about hegemony and the law that, on the one hand, encompasses everything and, on the other hand, is subject to political dissent. Insofar as one is never outside of the law, activism against it from within always already contains poetic formations. Moreover, insofar as alternative legal systems exist only potentially, these poetic formations are bound to spring from an understanding of the community of dogs as an effect of their being in the same space, yet not together.

Seen from a meta-discursive perspective, one can say that my own performing a work of criticism on texts under development and publication is as contradictory to the academic task at hand as anything: per definition you cannot write on texts that are both there and not there; also per definition, in institutionalized academic discourse, any non-linear thinking is 'bad' thinking, or more prosaically put, is 'poetry'. But this is where the aesthetics of the fragment becomes not only crucial but also instrumental to my scope: to show just how some of the mechanisms that underlie the workings of hegemonic discourse function, by analyzing drafts and unpublished material that emphasize hidden and undisclosed powers that can only be fathomed by bits and pieces, by fragments. The fragment is not only a residue, a remainder, or a detachment from a presupposed whole, but it can also be performed fragmentarily precisely as the fragment eludes linearity; a fragment, more often than not, has no beginning, no middle, and no end.

The fragment is always an opening unto potential. The point is that any hegemonic discourse can be uncovered by means of employing the dynamics of the fragment. As the following first poem from *Dogge Songs* illustrates. But first, "What I Wood Like To Be If I Wuzn't What I Am" – (in *Noose and Hook* this new linguistic idiom approaches even more the working of sounds, rather than those of the visual sign; thus the title acquires this form: "Whut i Wood Like To Bee If i Wuzn't What i am") – offers an aesthetic of the community that creates literary formations even when the community follows in resignation the law's dictates. The poem is a political manifestation, yet its poetic expression and aestheticism is not ignored. This means that Emanuel's community of dogs is identified as subversive in its very conformity to the hegemonic state. The truth that the dog narrator identifies and speaks of while contemplating the state of affairs together with its mistress is itself a subversive truth and as such marks the moment of barking as a moment of loss and dystopia. Writes Emanuel:

> We wuz unter dogs, she sd,
> *the US hast gone to the dogs*
> my mistrust sd,
> livin as we did amongst the abandoned furnitures
>
> in that overturnt rooms of der 21th C.
>
> altho i wast not displeased snurflin arount the feet of der tyrants,

nor thru the surroundin hills n hovels, nor the post-
apocolyptic fens n bogs;
I am a pastoral animal and this ist my past.

Howefer, sometimes when that liddle crease of sun
come thru the clouts
& wast scuffed out,
        & the wint blundered toward us,
& I wast readin the sightwalk fer the news
of all those who been here & who were gone,

I wisht I was a burt,
        to do a fly-over of this vale of tears,

the evenings I tried to discus this w/her. i would ask
*when wilt the spring come & the swans upon the rivers
w/ their coral beaks* but she't yawn & dowse the lamp
& the black ate us.

The moon lookt white & damp as a cut radish back
in the years of the radish;
in truth as i lay in the dark, spookt, i did not feel

the US hat gone to the dogs

        but to somethin that could take the colt
and dark & lovt it
                              like
an albatross or a worm,
or one of the other lower, meeker orders that

wilt inherit the earth.

The dog-speaker of this poem begins his observations by repeating what his mistress said, which emphasizes the nature of how hegemony works: through perpetuating itself as an ideology that rests not only on force but mainly on beliefs. A community marks its linguistic belonging either by obeying the dominant force as a result of having been coerced to do so or by accepting voluntarily new laws and ideas as they are passed off by the dominant code precisely as commonsensical. The commonsense that is the result of a one-sided act becomes thus ingrained in the community but only as an *impotential* state. What remains is whatever[3] has gone to the dogs. The dog in its singularity, while probing the commonsensical truth, namely, that it takes a community to enforce a hegemony, also shows bewilderment. When it wants to talk with its mistress about the implications of her claim regarding the decaying state of affairs in the US, the dialogue is interrupted as she puts out the light. The particularity of the rumor that the US has gone to the dogs is in the poem fleshed out as a potential. As such it is shared by word of mouth.

The subversive potential lies in the use of the catachrestic meaning of the idiomatic phrase that something 'has gone to the dogs' which is clearly meant to have a double signification for the dogs. What goes, or has gone to the dogs also means that the dogs get it, yet the dog in Emanuel's poem feels that insofar as he got nothing, then, the US must have gone to the lower orders, such as birds and worms. What the dog registers when pointing to the different hierarchies in its world is that one feels the power

---

3 Agamben employs the term "whatever" to designate not that which is indifferent but that which itself has been excluded and thus always returns. Deconstructing the Latin adjective *quodlibet* Agamben says: "the common translation of this term as "whatever" in the sense of "it does not matter which, indifferently" is certainly correct, but in its form the Latin says exactly the opposite: *Quodlibet ens* is not "being, it does not matter which," but rather "being such that it always matters." The Latin always already contains, that is, a reference to the will (*libet*). Whatever being has an original relation to desire" (Agamben, 1993: 1).

of hegemony when hegemony is at its highest ironical moment. For the dog-poet in particular, which Emanuel's dog undoubtedly is, domination is not only physical and symbolic, as political and cultural theorists would have (Gramsci, Bourdieu, Foucault), but also finds itself constantly in a potential state. It is this potentiality in a hegemonic state that determines the degree of dominance. Here I can give an example of what I mean by hegemony that operates with potentiality besides literal and symbolic orders by referring to the novelist Joseph Heller, for whom whatever has gone to the dogs is a community that is acquitted of intention and thus remains at the site of the unspeakable. Writes Heller in *Something Happened:*

> In the office in which I work there are five people of whom I am afraid. Each of these five people is afraid of four people (excluding overlaps), for a total of twenty, and each of these twenty people is afraid of six people, making a total of one hundred and twenty people who are feared of at least one person. Each of these one hundred and twenty people is afraid of the other one hundred and nineteen, and all of these one hundred and forty-five people are afraid of the twelve men at the top who helped found and build the company and now own and direct it. (Heller, 1974: 13)

Here Heller speaks of the notion of fear, but this fear is the kind of fear that the community agrees upon accepting in its potential state. The community thus partakes in the process of coercion. As a potential, hegemony can manifest itself through fear either literally or symbolically, but most of all it realizes itself beyond mere manifestation through the abolition of intent. Emanuel's dog's implicit question, 'what gives?' and equally implicit answer, 'nothing gives' reflected in the title whose hypothetical resonance calls for a *coming community,* to use Agamben's notion of the community that indicates linguistic belonging, is here paralleled by Heller's narrator who also goes on to ask the potential question, or the question of potentiality and its consequences for a community:

> What would happen if, deliberately, calmly, with malice aforethought and obvious premeditation, I disobeyed? I know what would happen: nothing. Nothing would happen [...] My act of rebellion would be absorbed like rain on an ocean and leave no trace. I would not cause a ripple. I suppose it is just about impossible for someone like me to rebel anymore and produce any kind of lasting effect. (19)

The question at stake in Emanuel's poem is not about how to reconcile the problem of hegemony with that of a dominated community, but about how to mediate between the actions identified with going against ideology and actions identified by their passive necessity. In other words, what does barking at the wrong doors do for that which potentially has gone to the dogs? – the dog in the poem never refers to anything concretely actualized, but as suggested earlier, it identifies a lack. The claim is that the dogs got the US but the dogs in question find this claim unsubstantiated. In contrast, in the revised version of this poem in *Noose and Hook* several aspects presented in draft form are upgraded to occupying a space of their own. Thus, this very phrase, "To the Doggs" – also the sppech act of "Dedication:" *To the Doggs* – wanders from the initial text to become part of an interior paratext in the final poem "Interior Mongrelogue." It thus gets the privilege to connote performatively and on several levels what the state of 'to the dogs' may implicate. The literal, metaphorical, but also metonymical significance of this phrase is thus intertwined within the internal workings of perception. This poem, rendered also in italicized letters, is now in its final version short, to the point, and more reflective of the relation dog/master, or rather object/subject than in the longer draft version.

> *An idea wiggles its ruffles at me.*
> *Thotfullness gropes for me.*
>
> *The nashun went to the dogs. Whut did it matter?*
> *i wuz a dogg? She was a leash wit out a dogg.*
> *i grew wags an lookt up at her.* (24)

Emanuel's insistence in *Noose and Hook* on using a non-capitalized form for the first person singular "i," when the dog refers to itself, suggests a concern with what conditions subjectivity especially when the subject, in this case the object 'dogg', not only sees itself objectified in relation to the master, the Subject, but also realizes that any perception of it as a dog (conventionally inscribed as a three-letter word), or as a dogg (unconventionally rendered as a four-letter word), or perhaps as something else entirely different ("whut does it matter?") matters none in power relations that are not symmetrical. Along these lines, one of the most valuable additions that Emanuel contributes to making the *Dogge Songs* more nuanced is in the use of suggested uncertainty about word-constructions. That is to say that many of the poems after establishing the conventional word and sound pattern of a phrase, directs the reader to considering how words can be comprehended beyond the otherwise problematic and often strained one-to-one relation, namely through the dictionary. Almost by performing an analytical philosophy gesture (à la Wittgenstein), structuralist construction (à la Saussure), and deconstructive dismantling (à la Derrida) Emanuel's "mongrelogues" deal with the question of naming and dissemination of meaning. In "How Dogg got its Name" in *Noose and Hook,* we read about the dog observing his mistress who is obviously in the writing and thinking profession – if writing and thinking can be thought of as such – as the tone of the poem also indicates. The dog under the table thus reports:

> Sittin in the booth she rote
> *Life iz borin tho we must not say so.*
>
> It's worst than that, i mutters
> under neath the table
>
> where the pages
> wit alfabets wuz hangin unto one
> an uther. Steppin out frum under neath
> those thunders i venturd, Whut r yew readin
> an writin about?
>
> About yew, she sd.
>
> Well, whut am i dubbed?
>
> Dogg, she sd. (23)

Paradoxically, what such constructions show is that although meaning is destabilized at the very moment when alphabets are thought of, it is precisely through the dissemination of other potential meanings that the same word might be a representation of, through supplements and traces, that symmetry can be restored where the enunciation of subject positions is concerned.

The poem "Tuff Times" – which is both a continuation, but also a fragment, or a detachment of the initial dogge song – demonstrates this further:

> We iz liven in mid evil an medicated times
> i sd to her,
>
> Make the best uf it.
> Get wit the program, sd i.
>
> *Which program iz that*
> *she wundered,*
>
> *doggs eatin doggs?*
>
> "dogg duz not eat dogg," iz the sayin, sd i.
>
> We spoke in this year in the 21st centuree
> amidst debt an tremble.
>
> Truble! She sd,
> Amidst debt and truble!
>
> i sd
>
> okaa-aay.
>
> Whut-ever. (26)

If in the initial draft the tough times of the dogs is not historically identified as such, in *Noose and Hook* it acquires a name: the Middle Ages (of the 21st century). What persists in both texts, and then throughout the whole of "The Mongrelogues" is the interesting imagery and idea that blackness, associated with the dark times of the plague, indentured slavery and the like, eats everything. This blackness can be read as a form of blind illiteracy from which a community cannot escape. In "The Mongrelogues," however, while the poems focus on the pastoral, they also suggest that illiteracy need not mean incapacity to engage with word-play: "i am a pastoral animal and this iz my past," concludes the dog in the final poem (36). In the draft form, the consequence of illiteracy takes the shape of a blind belief in the biblical promise which states that the meek shall inherit the earth. This promise is, however, only a potential that can never be actualized insofar as it disconnects the community's commitment to religious thought from the 'formal' awareness of hegemony.

The function of hegemony is to ensure that most people believe in the same things most of the time even when they use different languages to express it. There is thus not much space for dialogue. If talk is initiated by the dominated class, the dominating force will make sure to put out the light. Formal hegemony follows the formal law of the signifier, and as Derrida has shown, this law works with the substitution of signs and marks, intentional effect and intention (Derrida, 1998: 66). In Emanuel's mongrelogues a similar strategy of substitution between the kingdom that is to come and the one that has gone to the dogs is at work: while the meaning of the sign 'to come to inherit' is not dependent on the community's understanding of it; the effect of the mark left by a deteriorated political situation relies very much on the community's commitment to the question of belonging. Thus the protagonist dog meditates constantly on his belonging to a community that enforces itself by obeying a hegemonic potential that moves beyond identity and enlightenment.

The second poem in the draft *Dogge Songs*, "Homeless" leaves the territory of the observant dog and the passive community and moves out of the house, as it were. The dog leaves the house of his mistress and seeks freedom in the forest. The poem begins with the imperative: "Chymleys lend me your throats" and thus indicates a sense of urgency for the necessity of having barking articulate itself in language. As the next lines indicate:

> Chemin-de-fer
> for the long notes and nectars of my berkes
>
> a voice.
>
> Old letters send me your vowels.

This poem combines the desire for language, through which a community can also be said to exist, with the desire for having language contained by a specific discourse. Unlike the first poem that emphasizes transmission in its use of references to prophetic orders, the "Homeless" poem calls for more concrete transformations. But this call for transformation also remains in an unrealized state insofar as the desire for a home, for walls of containment, dominates the discourse. The dog's desire is to be latched back onto his mistress' bosom. Writes Emanuel:

> Houses, houses where are yr itches and latches
> so that
> I might sip and kiss them, slip into and bee them?
>
> Ocean, beneath the roof of what existence
> are yr nooks and niches,
> that I might succumb to them?

> Yards and gardens
> earth and dirt–
> dear blue contusions…
> Red hens, I follow yr bloody sunrise and set
> to the end of the day that wast my day.
>
> Dear rooms stalled in debt and fences,
> palest fronds of or fond reaches of bleached muslin, curtains
> and the droppéd coins of the rose petals.
>
> Rooks, lend me
> the crumbs of yr black bread
> so i might follow you into the forest. (Emanuel, 2006)

The total identification with the dominant force, the one that has the economic power to build the edifices that the dog wants to become, works here both as a warning but also as a nostalgic return to previous states. The struggle for diminishing class differences gets entangled in a discourse of marginalization that is guided by a ruthless division between those who have and those who have not. In this order, what is at stake is not a question about a belief in inheritance, heavenly or earthly, but about how to deal with surviving in a community that is defined by loss. The loss of property itself, therefore, transforms here into a longing and nostalgia for the days that were. The speaking dog wants to follow the hens' sunrise to the end of the day that was his. Yet, a return to such days can only happen through the back alleys, through chimneys, and through stalled rooms in which what is remembered is only the smell of curtains and petals and crumbs. The romantic desire to return to a community in harmony with nature, the desire to follow deep into the forest, is here conveyed with a tone that suggests impossibility. After having tried the relative safety under its mistress' dominant force, the dog now realizes that it cannot make it on its own in the forest, and the chicken and rook communities only contribute to making the dog feel more marginalized than before. Emanuel thus seems to indicate that if class struggle transforms its impetus into a discourse of marginalization and nostalgia for domination, even if domination is by nature and not by culture, then, the only thing that a community can hope for is that the off-beat effect of the future that runs parallel with the past and is thus contaminated by it, will also create an off-beat voice that is loud enough to produce a constant awareness of the fact that exclusion is possible wherever. The song about homelessness is here intended to work at the limits of the institutions and practices that the marginalized find themselves in.

Emanuel's third poem, "Dogge's Job" takes this limit to another level where the processes of transmission and transformation become a site of resistance. Insofar as domination that is disseminated at all internal levels makes resistance almost impossible, Emanuel's dog acts not on his own conviction but on behalf of what has been said by others. This distance turns the prophetic and nostalgic dog into a trickster dog. Only as a trickster can Emanuel's dog identify the unspeakable, the unrepresentable, the unsaid and the unbarkable and thus save the individual from the position he finds himself thrust into or "the degree zero of hegemony" as Douglas Litowits calls it, "where the individual's self-understanding merges with the dominant understanding" (Litowitz, 2000: 529). The dominant power's codes that become internalized by individuals as commonsense can only be cracked by "whatever," in Agamben's sense, or by the improper and the comic-sense. It is perhaps for this reason that Emanuel was thinking of Herriman's cartoon series, in which the dog is forever barking at whatever. Barking in Herriman's cartoons takes the form of a brick hurled by the mouse Ignatz over Krazy Kat's cranium. The brick always makes a lot of noise and this noise is represented in the cartoon both as anticipation and prevention. "The cat lives to hear it and Offisa Pupp lives to prevent it," as Andrew Arnold observes in his review of the recently re-published cartoons (Arnold, 2002: http). Herriman's influence on the poem is not only visual but also linguistic, insofar as Emanuel's poem, if read aloud, produces similar sounds that turn the poem's nostalgia into romantic comedy and prophesies into romantic farces. As the following lines from "Dogg's Door" (in *Noose and Hook*, "Door's House") suggest:

> They tolt me every dogg has its door.
>
> i walkt up to this one.
> i gnaw on the shues, i try on the howls.
>
> It wuz rainin, it wuz snowin
> upon the narrow hawses.
>
>> i bark at the undertakers.
>> an at the mellencollie howl uf the fraits.
>
> an at the mellencollie howl uf the fraits.
>
> Mistrust, i wuz wearee uf the struggle not to bee
> Dogg
>
> But now i yam yr dogg.
> I yam dawg uf the yard,
> leapin frantick an dootiful,

> like a publick fountain,
> like a piston rammin against the housin—
>
> leapin iz my steady job. (Emanuel, 2006)

In *Noose and Hook* there are a few variations in the language:

> Mistrust,
> i am wearee uf the struggle not to bee dogg
> as iron filings must wearee uf the magnut.
> But now i am yr dogg.
> I will bee dawg uf the yard!
> leapin frantic an dootiful,
> like a pub lick fountin,
> like a piston rammin against the housin—
> leapin iz my steddee job. (Emanuel, 2010: 25)

In this poem it is clear that resisting hegemony also implies a return to its promises. The dog returns to its mistress in spite of her dominance, and the irony of this return is captured in the first line: "every dogg has its door." Emanuel plays with another idiomatic expression that promises better days, such as the one that says that every dog has its day. The fact that the dog gets to have a door instead of a day symbolizes not only a return to but also re-entering the hegemonic order. The struggle outside it is stronger and more complicated than the one that makes the dog weary of being under its mistress' dominance. Yet the dog's attempt to re-ingratiate itself with the mistress through close body connection – its breast against hers – does not assure him a better position in the house. In fact the dog has to settle with being the yard dog. However, as the dog implicitly reasons, getting to bark at everybody and nobody in particular is also a job.

Now, while this poem does not end very optimistically, the cartoonish description of the dog barking at its own door or at "the undertakers" plays with intertextual references that recall at least two other texts besides the invocation of the hurling of bricks in Herriman's graphic world. Franz Kafka's short story, "The Refusal" depicts a small community of people that regularly gathers to plea with the local colonel and petition for small favors. The community never gets a positive reply, and it has grown so accustomed to the colonel's refusal that every time a rejection is received, it sighs with relief. As Kafka writes: "the citizens can always count on a refusal. And now the strange fact is that without this refusal one simply cannot get along" (Kafka, 1971: 267). Kafka's community almost rejoices in its identification with what is a *status quo* situation. It is precisely the immobile and rigid hegemony that enables the hurling of a brick or a dagger, even though the effect neither goes beyond the making of noise, nor does it get prevented fully by law officers. As Kafka writes "[o]ur officials have always remained at their posts" (263) thus describing the paradox of the unjust system that one submits to not because it is unjust but because it is stable in its refusal to incorporate alternative states.

The other text that Emanuel's barking dog brings to mind is Theodor Herzl's well known Zionist manifesto *The State of Israel*, where he makes the claim that even if the Jews "were a nation of undertakers – such as absurdly exaggerated accounts make [them] out to be – [they] should not require another nation to live on" (Herzl, 1943: 17). The contrast here is between the educated Jews who, while cultured, also speak a vernacular language – which emphasizes their dependence on a nation state that is not their own – and the uneducated dogs who, while showing loyalty and submission to the ones who own them, also speak a 'dogolect' that has a subversive potential. The 'dogolect' here comes to represent the "cult of the vernacular," to use Gavin Jones's expression, insofar as it cannot be improved on or dictated by the social elite. As Jones puts it, with the rise of interest in American dialects, a fear of too much contamination was also growing: "a language that remains in touch with the nation's diverse cultural groups is a chaotic threat to the coherence of cultural authority [...] Dialect could incite a sense of linguistic anarchy and social fragmentation as easily as it could suggest a national distinctiveness based on a popular vernacular" (Jones, 1999: 15).

Emanuel's dog-talk is represented through her use of eye-dialect which, while no different in terms of lexis and syntax from English, indicates that the one who speaks it, while occupying an inferior position, also has power. The sentences that have an 'of' construction, the 'of' being written on the page as 'uf', clearly suggest this dual position of belonging and barking. Words such as 'mellencollie' actually play with lexis, suggesting a transformation from an adjective ('melancholy') into a noun referencing the dog breed collie.

These intertextual references to texts that have had an impact in terms of the effects of their hurling rhetorical daggers at irritating parties and making a lot of noise suggest again that ultimately whatever has gone to the dogs, even if only in theory, still means that the dogs get it. The disenfranchised community becomes enfranchised as long as it speaks not only in multiple but also contaminated tongues; as we have it in the allusions to the archaic middle English, dialects, and Herriman's cartoons in which particularly the cat occupies a marginalized position both linguistically and socially; the cat speaks English with an accent and does the unacceptable, which is to fall in love with a member of another community, and who is also of a lower species. Herriman's policing dog mediates with its swinging club between the cat's affectionate throwing of bricks at Ignatz, and Ignatz's verbal stabbing at the cat's ignorance. Herriman's dog thus embodies the hegemony that brings the coming community together, by uniting the eloquent with the less articulate. While old ideas thus become relevant for new ones, new ideas correct the old ones. Herriman's dog not only embodies whatever it takes for the community to function, but also speaks whatever.

By letting the dog speak 'whatever,' Emanuel's new idiom that combines the archaic with the accented is what marks the community of dogs a coming community, which means that the community is neither particular, nor general, neither individual, nor generic. As such, the community's answer to hegemony is that hegemony itself is always already predicated on the workings of whatever, and hence moves towards its own taking-place, towards the idea of power.

But power is, however, articulated against a defeatist, pessimistic, fatalistic, and deterministic background. This can be seen clearly in the lines "we iz livin in the mid evil and medicated times" in "Tuff Times," a poem that plays on the words medieval and evil, also suggesting a sense of smell and taste. This indicates that varieties beat periods. Although dogs are more into bones, they can smell a thing or two; they can smell the coming of 'medicated' time and thus anticipate its drowsiness. Clearly the dog has no other choice than to go with 'whatever,' as the last line in "Tuff Times" has it. Whatever the program or the time is, it doesn't matter. There is thus a tensioned movement from the potential that 'whatever' holds towards accepting a situation to the dynamics of rejection that closes potential around a defeatist situation.

And yet, where there is movement there is also displacement, which means that power as an idea can be inherited by all orders, high and low, and these orders can either centralize it or marginalize it, pass it down or lose it. Just as the dog is a domestic animal, so is hegemony. Emanuel's language, with its persuasive alliterations and compelling rhyme schemes – both in the draft form, where the dogs articulate their predicament through singing songs, and "The Mongrelogues" in *Noose and Hook,* where the same is articulated more through interior monologue – produces a rhetoric of passing in the sense of inheriting whatever; namely that which always matters, or that which is never indifferent. Letters such as k, q, and w, insistently recurrent in all the poems discussed here, indicate a tone which suggests that communities spelled with Ks or Qs acquire a voice as Woice that lends a dog's barking a dagger. What cannot be inherited in heaven or on earth shall be willed away as whatever. The final poem, "Dead Dogg," in "The Mongrelogues," (the draft version) makes a strong statement about passing through electrocution, as the dogg informs us: "i took 2000 volts." A very powerfully subliminal "k"-sound here is meant to have the same effect on the reader, who finds herself in a state of having been electrocuted, but while the dog dies, its ghost persists, as the instructive and didactic last lines of the poem indicate: *"Look up Zeitgeist & it sez see Tide. See Ghost."*

Although this poem was dropped from the final version of *Noose and Hook* in the sections that follow after "The Mongrelogues," the Ghost hovers, is free of constraints, and thus has the potential to see more, learn more, and haunt more. The pulverized and immaterial dog thus reappears alongside Modernist writers and philosophers, postmodern poets, suicidal critics, and painters; all eating, drinking, and sitting in comfortable furniture. This is the age of design, conceptual revisions of language, and the writing about objects in the face of the impossibility to be a subject as such, after wars and after dissolutions. After the *Dogge Songs,* in *Noose and Hook* the Ghost says, "Hello!"

GREETING

> *In this most Christian of worlds*
> *All poets are Jews.*
> —MARINA TSVETAYEVA

> *What is the difference between pleasure in the whole or not pleasure,*
> *pleasure in the half.*
> *What is the difference between pleasure and a pleasure.*
> —GERTRUDE STEIN

In a now famous formulation, Thodore Adorno claimed that after Auschwitz writing poetry is impossible. He forgot the food. Emanuel's *Noose and Hook* (2010) is an astonishing reminder of the fact that poetry, like love, passes through the stomach. This means to say that if we can get our hands on food, we can create. The first poem – after a poem epigraph about being in the belly of a beast, like Jonas – is all about depicting food and drinks, and can be read as a foreword to the very idea of 'after'. What there is 'after' is eating and atmosphere as clearly suggested in these key words: Martinis, fillets, sandwiches, butter, silky coffee, T-bones, coconut, eggs, Stilton cheese. The last lines, "Noir, Hello" can be read as a full stop after a heavy meal indeed, but also as a salutatory opening towards a sense of renewed energy that prepares the reader for experiencing more of what comes 'after' and what is potentially unidentifiable, as if suggesting that when all the problems in the world are forgotten, at least for a while, as the poem puts it: "it's a good thing we're tough. It's a hard and dirty world" (5). The relationship between eating and objects as vehicle for revaluing subjectivity is further explored in a final structural complementarity. The last poem in *Noose and Hook* ends with the same "Hello," after repeating the title. Thus the phrase "Noir, Hello" in the first poem, becomes more concrete in the last poem as "Noose and Hook, Hello." What this last poem also suggests is that the mediating vehicles between thinking and eating are objects. Objects are addressed as in a diary, and we come full circle in terms of how poetic genres are also mediated through formal approaches to writing: through pastiche, imitation, letters, journals, poetry, prose poetry and so on. The endearing words "Dear Noose, Dear Necktie, Dear Cravat," thus constitute gestures of salutation, which, again, emphasize an intimate atmosphere, but one in which something happens in terms of action, or silent action, and in terms of self-awareness as the reader catches herself reading, and the writer catches herself writing.

Considering the poems in *Part One*, the idea is that after eating, if poetry is not possible, then laughter certainly is, as the lines in the epigraph, a poem by Ted Hughes, indicate. Criticism is also possible, or above all criticism in the form of quotation and paraphrase, as the poems in this first section suggest, poems that find a fuller resonance in the last poems that constitute the third and final part of the book. After criticism, dreaming is allowed. The beginning poems that initiate the volume are followed by the larger section in the middle, "The Mongrelogues" – Emanuel's reworked dog-poems from the *Dogge Songs*. These have different styles: the first is a descriptive prose poem, but one which also reads as a poem with run-on lines. As it is also flushed to the right on the page, it can be seen as a second or rather as a third epigraph, given that the whole volume is initiated by a poem called "My Life." This poem can be regarded both as a foreword, but also as an epilogue to the whole work. In the notes to the *Noose and Hook* Emanuel credits Robert Lowell for the style, which she "imitates," as she puts it. Although she does not mention it anywhere in this final version, particularly Lowell's poem called "Epilogue" is evoked. In the draft version Emanuel used two lines from it: "All's misalliance / Yet why not say what happened?" Here one would like to believe that the reason why these lines vanished from *Noose and Hook,* is because Emanuel found herself engaged in performing a gesture towards marking an elliptical understanding, as it were. If all is misalliance, then, if writing happens, it can only happen at the expense of either creating gaps or allowing for other voices to be embodied in one's own words. There can be only imitation, or a depiction of portraits in one's own image, yet an image that is crafted through the perception of oneself as seen through the eyes of others.

The second poem in *Part One* suggests this much. It can be said to function as a pastiche of Hughes's personification of laughter: "still laughter scampers around... / And rolls back onto the mattress, legs in the air / But it's only human / and finally it's had enough – enough!" In Emanuel's rendition, Hughes's short repetitive and cadenced lines above become means for framing a tableau. We thus read in the last two stanzas: "I sat and smoked and lingered. / Inside me a murder sulked and ached / like a lake behind a dam. I was waiting until the world was on my side / and would turn itself murderous for my sake" (Emanuel, 2010: 7).

There is good symmetry at work between *Part One* and *Part Three*, as Emanuel, after detouring through considering other possibilities for the condition for the existence of subjectivity in the anthropomorphization of dogs, or rather by decentring the "andro" in the human, follows more explicitly into the footsteps of writers whose trademarks can be said to have been the smashing to pulverization of received ideas about poetry, poetics, and criticism.

By way of making reference to a letter, Emanuel, through a dialogic gesture, depicts not only the ghost of Walter Benjamin haunting Baudelaire, but also Benjamin's concrete, analytical, and at the same time evaluative letter to Baudelaire, and then, finally, herself in the poem "Dream In Which I Meet Myself." What is thus suggested in this tripartite structure is that there is always another layer of 'things' that we can add to cognitive, emotional, rational, and 'cosmic' dimensions of consciousness. There is always a portrait of a meta-self that emerges out of any act of pulverisation. This much is suggested already at the level of the paratext, in the title to the whole volume, *Noose and Hook*. Quite literally, after annihilation and pulverisation something else begins to emanate out of the ashes. It is a sort of nothingness that caries with it a radical commitment to something. For Emanuel, it is challenging to think in terms of reinventing new ties, loops, and fastenings around nothingness, or around pulverized portraits.

Thus, Emanuel's way of investigating not only into what conditions the existence of something out of nothing, but also into how something moves is by way of recasting poetry as a fragment. In this sense, it is not accidental that in the final pages of the volume she chooses to paraphrase Walter Benjamin who dedicated his whole life to making a reality his dream of creating an entire body of criticism consisting only of quotations. His monumental and at the same time momentous *Passagen-Werk (The Arcades Project)* (accumulated between 1927 and 1940) testifies to this very possibility. What Emanuel seems to identify in her poem about Benjamin's encounter with Baudelaire is the power of the prophetic vision of both these writers about overcoming the impossibility of writing. Benjamin makes a clear gesture towards suggesting that after atrocities, if the streets, with their opening onto seeing food and smell poetically, are not enough for inspiration, then other things may be enough. Furniture is mentioned, which, again, recalls for us the potential that furniture has to act as a vehicle for mediation between tensioned spaces. As Charles Simic puts it in a definition I referred to earlier: "The prose poem is a burst of language following a collision with a large piece of furniture."

In Emanuel's poem, "April 18, the 21st Century, Cher Baudelaire" in which Benjamin's "Charles Baudelaire: A Lyric Poet in the Era of High Capitalism" is referred to, Emanuel already performs a gesture of ventriloquism that imitates the academic discourse of the 19th century: descriptive titles that disclose the genre and often also either sum up an entire thesis, or indicate affection or love. The speaker in this poem is however on more familiar tones with the addressee than the presumed anonymous long-bearded old professors. This is a poem of great beauty and it conveys many Romantic and sublime feelings. But it is also a poem conscious of what it does: robbing itself of its metaphors and pointing to the power of quoting, quite similar to the power of prophesying. As a prophet one does not speak in one's own voice. One ventriloquizes the one who is always silent. Thus, the poem begins:

> Cher Baudelaire,
>
> Tonight as I boarded my train of thought and entered the third class compartment of my mind, I thought of Margaret Atwood who wrote: "I am in love with Raymond Chandler because of his interest in furniture." Baudelaire, I am no one but the insatiable identity descending upon me and tonight it is yours. I've thought, if Baudelaire were not Baudelaire I would be Baudelaire, though in truth I have thought the same about Walter Benjamin when he says (I paraphrase), "I am in love with Baudelaire because of his interest in furniture. When writing about furniture Baudelaire is free from capitalism's philosophy and history and archeology and is enthralled by upholstery, and this is a way of thinking and being that is wholly new in the world and was made so by Baudelaire."
>
> No quotation is innocent. Every act of quotation is an act of ventriloquism. Every ventriloquism is an usurpation. (52)

How does one get from furniture to portraits? The ones that are not about conveying the spirit of what is depicted, but the spirit of materiality, as it were, the color and pattern of upholstery? This is the question that preoccupies Emanuel. In her style – this is a prose poem that fills some three pages – she returns to the idea of objects being able to contain other objects, and with them their material souls. Particularly the poem "inside gertrude stein" is alluded to, as there is the same feeling and tone in the conversational style that suggests both horror but also adoration of the idea of being subsumed by another's genius. Referencing the literary and historical criticism on Baudelaire that accounts for his writing as having been done mainly out of ignorance of his cultural environment, philosophy, archeology, physiology, art history, here, in this poem, according to the claims of Maxime du Camp and also Benjamin, Emanuel's speaker thus further exclaims:

> How lucky you are, cher Baudelaire, to have found me to shelter you, to have found the succulent hallways of my lines, and the shimmering windows of my tropes, and the sticky navels of the little hash pipes I have left lying about for you, the ease, the comfort, the respite my verse provides you. Or maybe not. I sit on my train and watch capitalism struggle in the windows. In the city of the mind the great alcove of night closes over us. Even over you, Baudelaire, who invented a world that had never before existed – a completely interior world of upholstery without philosophy – and in so doing gained the undying envy of the future Walter Benjamin who was sentenced to live inside a world outside and who, therefore, ironically, tried to save himself from that world and its history by committing suicide at Hotel de Francia in Port-Bou in September of 1940. (52-54)

This poem is not just about pulverizing thought – first class or third class – but about the consequence of having thought pulverized by images of a new world. Benjamin committed suicide not because he was unable to see this new world but because he did not believe in it. Thus the portraits that Emanuel depicts of Benjamin and Baudelaire are portraits which, while in dialogue with each other, are also about anticipating a world in which moments are captured in a snap, or are frozen at the moment when the *geist* gives up its ghost, as it were. The role of the poet-speaker here is to be ready to take a photograph of the philosopher in his newly upholstered armchair. In Charles Simic's book, *The Metaphysician in the Dark,* there is a similar view of such a world that ends *Noose and Hook.* Says Simic: "'Such is the photograph, it cannot say what it lets us see', writes Roland Barthes. Still, the silence of the image invites a dialogue, or rather an attempt at ventriloquism" (Simic, 2003: 19).

How to capture the ventriloquism of a pulverized world? This is the other question that Emanuel seems to ask by implicating herself in the dream of a dog. In the poem "Dream in which I meet Myself" – the first poem of *Part Three* – 'seeing' things transcends the prophetic and turns into action. There is a dialogue between the dreamer, a narrator, and the dream itself. Thus we are told: "The dream tells us: She is still a servant. Even here" (38). Then the voice of another takes over and we have this physical description of eyes, or rather, seeing, in the first person: "My eyes fidget and scratch. / And then I see myself: I am this dream's dog. I want out" (38). One way out is through language. The section "The Mongrelogues" is thus ended, with more dogs gnawing and barking at the world around them.

Part Three invites the reader to consider action as a result of dialogue, which *Part Two* emphasizes, and begins with two telling epigraphs. One, a dialogue from Samuel Beckett's *Waiting for Godot:* "ESTRAGON: I can't go on like this. VLADIMIR: That's what you think." And another from Baudelaire's "The Faithful Dog": "Take me with you, and out of our joint misery we will make a kind of happiness." Paradoxically however, as these two epigraphs ironically reference, on the one hand, the frustration with waiting, and on the other, the not so immediate potentiality and promise of a happier world, they manage to establish an almost dreamlike world where action is only possible as a way of bypassing first-order agency. Action happens in quotation marks, in parenthesis, by way of dedicating, by way of recording memories in a journal, or by way of defending oneself in a courtroom. The action in *Part Two,* which relies on testimony and evidence, is here continued by means of laying the cards on the table. *Noose and Hook* goes circular and ties its ropes not around closure but around potentiality. "Hello" can be read both as a greeting, but also as an act of admonishing, as in, 'hello, are you listening to what I've been saying?'

As suggested previously, the dog monologues, mongrelogues, or songs, which form *Part Two* – a middle section composed as a play in two acts – can be read as an autobiographical account of a life which is seen not only from a dog's perspective, but also from the position where an embodiment of 'dog' occurs, both in time and space. The epigraph from Langland is retained, as in the draft version of the work, "Thi dogge dar nat berke," but is now accompanied by a line from George Herriman: "Folkses Pipples – Wit your Kine Pimmchin – I will Sing the song of Songs," and another from Ferdinand Pessoa: "I multiplied myself to feel myself." This part is initiated by a table of contents, a description of the *dramatis personae* involved in the play, such as the main protagonist, Dogg, his mistress, a policeman, the court interrogators; a description of cameo appearances from Langland, Herriman, Pessoa, John Berryman, John Wycliff, and Rachel DuPlessis; and descriptions of setting, action, and time. The Action is suggested by way of summing up, such as the titles of the 'action' poems indicate: "Dogg is lost, Is found, Meets Mistrust, Has a Day, Endures, Hard Times, Snarls, Is Abandoned, Forsaken, Arrested, Interrogated, And Meditates Upon the World." The Time is left open unto potentials, yet in a conclusive manner: "No Time like the Present" (19-20).

This *Table of Contents* thus already establishes a set of relations which – as suggested previously in the discussion of the three "dogge poems" of the initial draft – are meant to destabilize not only hegemony but also subjectivity. The whole setting for these poems conjures a *noir* atmosphere, or that of alienation, which parallels life in the US in many remote places. These places can, however, also be said to be cosmopolitan. The mongrelogues describe the life of an anthropomorphized dog who experiences the second world war, but more precisely from a canine, rather than andro-perspective of a dog as such; if such a perspective is possible, notwithstanding. This very possibility is at the heart of this quite literally central section in the book. The 40s are recalled and a *noir* scene is also set. In "Stray Dog" we read these beginning lines whose tone persists throughout the whole act: "i wuz following a boat / down the avenew / the smell of wet meat clung to it / leapin over ashes and trashes / wit out a license [...] i thot this iz the life - / a planet uf ruin an disorder and the dogs of the world runnin the world [...] "We haf gone to the dawgs," / I heard sum one saying." / There wuz a door open / I went into it" (21-22). The harsh sounds provided by the added second 'g' in 'dog,' the zeds and the fs emphasizing the go between strong voicing and hushing, alert the reader to the seriousness of the situation. In other words, when the speaker says 'dog', she means 'dog'.

This dog perspective, which initiates a cycle of dog-lamentations by picking up the tone of transformation from the poem which ends *Part One,* called "Metamorphosis," – a poem inspired by Kafka's story that carries a line from Kafka as an epigraph: "What's happened to me? He thought" (16) – suggests a parallel to the absurdist and Kafkaesque universe in which things happen beyond human logic. The Kafka epigraph recalls Robert Lowell's line in his "Epilogue": "All's misalliance. Yet why not say what happened?" which served as inspiration for the final version of *Noose and Hook*. In "Metamorphosis" the speaker does not only undergo a physical change into a dog, but also a linguistic one. Not only is this poem more clearly a prose poem than were the ones in "The Mongrelogues" – which have short and concise lines – but it is also highly articulated and philosophical. After the speaker in the poem realizes her transformation, she begins to notice what she can do in and with the newly acquired body. Thus we read lines which combine considerations about mind and matter:

> My nose became an organ of thoughtfulness, my ears were shells
> in which the seas of the voices of the world thrashed and
> Night fell, day rose, the old died, the young went on.
> [...] The voices of the masters perched above us said, *you are just a gregarious piece of furniture.*
> The war came and went beyond the bars of my life. I was dog.
> Then I embraced it.
> Then I was undone and replaced it (16-17).

What is new in this poem – which is also a poem strategically positioned between *Part One* and *Part Two* to emphasize precisely a transitory movement which is taken over in "The Mongrelogues" with the dogs roaming the streets and thinking, almost acting out an Aristotelian peripatetic walk – is the idea that all things enter in a relation of misalliance with one another. As objects are anthropomorphized and streets given a specific gender, human subjects literally emerge as thinking animals, thus suggesting an eternal return of the same, a life cycle in which, while things change, they also stay the same. "Metamorphosis" begins ironically with this dialectics of the standstill: "As for myself – wherever there was a street going indifferently about her business, I was the dog" (16).

But what metamorphosis is, is precisely a meta-relation. Emanuel's use of the idea of transformation is a way of enabling a return to what has been pulverized either by war – the second world war is mentioned via a return to Gertrude Stein, whose statement: "now, we have an occupation" (13) acquires in Emanuel a meta-resonance – or relies on language constructions. The latter also undergo metamorphoses, yet language constructions can always be placed in a symmetrical relation to what potentially can happen. Language and language-based games can point to the existence of hypothetical 'other' worlds, such as a dog world may be. Emanuel's shifting between real and fictitious worlds and idioms is an attempt to precisely answer the Kafkaesque, ominous question: "What happened to me?" We find a correlate to the idea of being occupied or invaded by formal language constructions in *Part Three* in an untitled prose poem.

The absence of a title is however made present in the very first line: "I tried to flatter myself to extinction; tried to bury alive in a landslide of disparagement ego and subjectivity and the first person pronoun singular" (43). This poem consists almost entirely of an attempt to stab language, and kill off grammar. The misalliance between word and image consists of meta-considerations of the poetics of poetry, particularly as the speaker of the poem tries to circle the square, as it were. Enforce subjectivity by numbers. But as numbers belong to a form of more artificiality – all math operates with symbols – what is suggested is that all meta-levels are abstract levels *par excellence*. This poem operates on a discursive level with performing not only the sentence, yet by killing the sentence off, but also with performing a gesture towards acknowledging what grammar and syntax do for establishing an identity not only for the poet but also for the poem. Thus we read:

> I ran identity to ground with the dogs of irony; I tried to kill, bury, burn, embalm and erase the outlines of me, mummify myself in the damp wrappings of surrealism, sever and rearrange me with Stein's cubism, break, buy, bribe, drive a stake through me; tried to whip to death the whole frumpish horse-and-buggy, essentialist, runs-in-the-blood notion I had of who "I" was; like Stein I tried to bleed the bloody paragraph to death, the bloody sentence, killed the semicolon with the machete of my wit, tried to censor and edit, rewrite and emend me, my belief in lifeblood, marrow, core, and fiber. (43)

These lines not only operate with the aesthetics of the fragment as ruin – which is seen as liberating – but they also point to the tyranny of formal constructions. Drawing on earlier philological criticism, which insisted on the preservation of linguistic constructs that clearly demarcate who the agent is in a phrase, or who is doing what to whom, Emanuel here, by asking questions as to the function of the "I," also eradicates the sentence that the "I" controls and has under its gaze. Thus the question "why is I having to keep its eye peeled, its eye on the ball, trying to steer…?" usurps the position of the "I" always in the Panopticon observing and passing sentence on the sentence.

The poem further actively considers the notion of silence – once the sentence is dead, what then? – precisely as an example of misalliance with words on a page. Here, not only is the reader considered – and the fact that reading is different than writing in the sense that it is more challenging as it requires that the brain decodes its own mystery of going about things where imagination is concerned – but also the writer/reader who has both skills activated: the psychology of reading and the concreteness of writing given through learned formulas. Here, the poet, who is also a reader of Philip K. Dick, who appears in the poem – is a teacher of creative writing as well, who takes the task of teaching seriously. As another untitled poem further towards the end of *Part Three* puts it:

> I told my student Kimber Lester, if you cannot actually write
> a poem at least write a sentence to tell me why
> in the eighth stanza of this *text* the image of a bloody dagger
> hangs before me?
>
> [...]   Consider that
> 1.   in this image of the bloody dagger
> 2.   buried in this hard dark scab of line
> 3.   in this densely botched moment of your personal life
> 4.   which has gathered its sense & meaning unto itself like a scar
> 5.   your life has got itself swallowed in an obscurity as deep
>   as the locked suitcase.
>
> Perhaps you could "unpack it."
>
> Now it is too late. You are gone into your lives,
> Caleb the Morose, Jennifer the Moat, Kimber
> smoking beneath the poured lavas of new scars.
> & somewhere in that dark airport lies
>
> my poem in which the electricity gives out & my husband
> & I lighting ourselves with the pale weeping of candles
> & an heretical manner of copulation set the duvet on fire,
> lies the obscure room & my inexplicable weeping. (49-50)

What Emanuel does in this poem, as in all the poems in *Part Three*, is denounce the workings of 'sentencing', both in a grammatical but also a judicial sense, by pointing to the irony of the situation: one sentences the sentence to death by phrasing the penalty as a written sentence. As this poem suggests – by juxtaposing a situation in which a poem about poetics is lost in some airport in Finland, and hence it is unreadable but can be reconstructed by means of writing sentences without sentences in it, which puts the students on a track where they can learn the craft of other elements that make up a sentence – is that form comes before all else. And if form comes before content, then, writing is possible all the time, after any time, of war or worship. There is thus a reason why the poems in this section invite the reader to consider not only misalliance, but also to perform a moment of listening to "what happened" so that another story can emerge. And as Emanuel suggests, such a story has to come out of struggle, absence, activism, evaluation, perception. Especially the poems which are untitled perform at the level of content the poet's desire to write or rather create titles *in absentia,* as it were, for topics on and around ellipsis, on and around subjectivity and ontology, on and around portraiture, on and around metaphysics, on and around that which cannot be expressed, on and around the unnamable.

In one of the first poems, Emanuel writes in an elegiac manner about personal experiences. She departs for a moment from the desire to create a close proximity with the reader, even when such proximity is emphasized. She makes clear, again, that all professions, even that of a writer or reader are linked to external factors, to form. Form is internalized, to be sure, but there are always different strategies and methodologies that create epistemic values for how we get to know what we know. What we get to know from reading poetry is that there will always be at least two sides to the story. All abstraction and reduction to form has two sides. Thus, what is suggested is that perhaps arithmetics, pure counting should feature more prominently in the process of attaining not only knowledge, but also self-knowledge. One of the more insightful propositions and challenging mystery of the oracle at Delphi, one that has been passed down to poets and people, "Know thyself," is that only by counting one's ways of getting to know things, including the intuitive ones, can one arrive at some form of enlightenment. Such ways are identified in this poem by means of recalling the materiality of the sign, the invention of the book, and the invention of putting sentences together so that some of them may even end up sounding prophetic, thus transcending the sensation of immediate certainty given through material signs. Thus says Emanuel:

> Personal experiences are chains and balls
> fatally drawn to the magnetic personality.
> And yet I have always been a poet
> who poured herself into the shrouds
> of experiences' tight dresses so that a reader could try to get
> a feel for the real me, metaphorically speaking, of course
> using only the mind, of course, and a dictionary
> which the mind wears like a surgical glove.
>
> [...] I hear the call to rise out of the trance of myself
> into the surcease of the dying world,
> Then it went dark. Real dark. Like snow. (9/11 witness.)
>
> I will never again write from personal experience.
> Since the war began I have discovered

(1) My life Is Unimportant and (2) My Life Is Boring.
But now, as Gertrude Stein wrote from Culoz in 1943,
Now, we have an occupation. (12)

What is announced here in a poststructuralist and postmodernist gesture – when writing is made aware of itself, of its being writing according to invented perceptions enabled by 'knowing' words – is that a writer, a reader, and a teacher of both, writing and reading, will always experience a feeling of being invaded. One's own subjectivity is pulverized, not in the wake of formalism but mainly in the wake of awakening the ghosts. The poem "The Occupation" picking up the *geist* of Gertrude Stein, reads:

> I used to love reading the great poets and the words that hovered like bees at the lines' cut edges scythed by their commas. But tonight, beyond my locked door, the ground takes charge of caving in. Somewhere the windows in kitchens smolder and soldier onwards toward a glass of gin. I long for its coffin, the heat of its sleep. Dear Sleep, help me sheet the furniture in the rooms of the brain. I will not look underneath at the black ache of the table or wake the furnishings into breathing. I will cut open the vein that feeds the beat of the pendulum. I once read the great poets until my heart was blown open. Now whenever I stoop over the hard desk of my heart – the soldiers come. Troy is burned. (14)

There is thus a struggle with how to reinvent oneself against the background of genius and greatness which crushes one sublimely by letting words fall into form like heavy avalanches. What Emanuel suggests is that writing as a formal enterprise, after the sweep of smashing wars of words or weapons, can only take place in the ellipses, as ellipses, in the silence of the white page. This white page is yet contaminated by its own fluttering, by allowing words to cross it, by being invaded without a chance to talk back, or enter a dialogue, not even with itself or the great poets. The beauty of Helen of Troy emerges out of subjectivity burnt on paper. But this Helen knows herself and what she is good at beyond ashes. She can re-decorate, move the furniture about, and push chairs.

The poem that precedes "The Occupation," an untitled poem, thematizes not only the problem with a pulverized image of the self as a whole 'text' but also with the potential of fragments to emerge out of a clearing. These fragments can be said to be sentences cut off from the whole, yet heavy and pregnant with meaning, both literally but also, again, judicially. The subject is sentenced to beauty, if what the subject has been through is the fire of poetry. The poem has these lines in it:

> Into the clearing of...
> she climbed and stood
>
> up from the black boots of her blackouts
> into her body.
>
> [...] A fever wrote the sentence
> and screwed it tight with ache
>
> and the long hair of the grass grew silvery and weak,
> lay greasily against the skull of dirt.
>
> My mother was a figure armed with...
> and came toward me

> flew to me as though I were a sentence
> that must be mended, that must be broken,
>
> then ended, ended, ended. (10-11)

Identifying the predicament of being lost, detached, or an eluded object, Emanuel's speaker in another untitled poem, likens her situation of having to navigate through formalist approaches to language through emotional and personal experience to that of painters who also have their battles to fight. Alluding to all the 'isms' that painting as a genre has gone through, also always being at the mercy of taste-makers and gate-keepers, what she laments is the *topos* of the site where the creative *geist* has found embodiment, namely in television. We are thus back to reconsidering the world of the image, but as it moves itself on screen. As such, the image is more impersonal, which has implications for the potential of the image to move others, than merely move itself. But whatever images the painter or the poet creates, what is ultimately valued is the community she creates within that becomes part of herself. Emanuel's speaker in this poem is as preoccupied with occupying a space among the painters as she was in the previous example where other poets invaded her own creativity, by becoming 'nominals' in a sentence. After the question: "What are people anyway but nouns?" she contemplates:

> I love the painters yawning and drifting in their black leather jackets in whose seams the toothed zippers grin. I have become a dog in their pack. I love being a dog in their pack. We are cogs in the assembly line of war and death. Smoke rises from a cigarette. Our pack thrusts its dark brooding towards the idea of a bonfire of the arts. *Turn back!* I want to cry. But the painters are saying painting itself is like a fire dying down to ash and smoke and being sucked

up into the chimney of Nothingness! Beyond our windows the moon floats through the greasy oceans of infinitude, *la mer infinite et graisseuse,* and the painters are peering into their latest installation in which they are drowning in a barrel of water someone screaming on a TV screen. The painters say they are trying to save the body by getting rid of the body and turning it into television! They want to unbecome it, so that it is like snow at four in the morning when the programming is over. Just say No to X! No to Y! No to the chromosome, the bones, the hairy and fibrous stuff of the material world! And *Yes* to art's program of ardent forward movement to the abyss. I am not so sure what to say about this so I say *What would happen if we turned back?* But the painters say this TV needed terror to be placed in. And now there is no back to turn to. (45-46)

The symmetrical relations that are established in this poem, between image and moving image, nouns and syllables, nothingness and grapheme, question and rhetorical question are meant to emphasize that every act of unbecoming is already a state of being. Things are as they are, and therefore it is understandable if anyone wants to have a say in it. The painters say this, the poets say that, and the war makers arbitrate without deliberation. And it is all happening on TV.

On a contextual level, the obvious question that emerges, yet one which no one can answer, is this one: how it is possible that those who wage war, commit crimes of genocide and terrorism, get away with it? Emanuel here seems to nod in approval at philosophers who take the discourse on ethics and morality to a higher level where what is considered is precisely the subject as a pulverized subject, the subject as a fragment that is the result of both sums, the sum of all convergences but also the sum of all divergences.

Giorgio Agamben, following Carl Schmitt, posits the notion that political concepts, at their base, are secularized theological concepts. This has implications for the way in which we think of the *homo sacer*, the accursed man – who according to a Roman law, once banned cannot be killed (in any act of sacrifice), but will always remain without rights – and sovereignty particularly where the relations: subject against subject and subject against object are concerned. When Agamben claims in his essay on Hannah Arendt, "Beyond Human Rights," that the "so-called sacred and inalienable rights of man prove to be completely unprotected at the very moment it is no longer possible to characterize them as rights of the citizens of a state" (Agamben, 2000: 19–20) he says something of significant consequence for the way in which we thematize free will[1].

While it is easy to imagine that governments today, when thinking about going to war, pick and choose as if they were at a supermarket, the complexity of the situation arises when one has to define who the enemy is, especially when the enemy is not in a symmetrical relation with the way in which human rights are defined. If the 'other' is a concept, rather than a subject, than even the act of witnessing the annihilation of an idea becomes preposterous. In the face of thinking that just because one does not have a well defined enemy, one can afford to invent things and then go to the supermarket and get the bullets according to the invention, particularly Schmitt's idea that "everything must

---

1 There is also a revised version of Agamben's essay under the title: "Biopolitics and the Rights of Man," in his work, *Homo Sacer: Sovereign Power and Bare Life*, where he develops more fully the idea of the subject whose status in the law is that of an exile.

be forced to the extreme so that it can be overturned out of a dialectical necessity" (Schmitt, 1988: 59) is relevant to consider.

In the context of *Noose and Hook*, by undoing subjectivity, or undoing the notion that the "I" is or can be in control all the time even when the "I" is shown to be beside itself, Emanuel offers a critique of capitalism, not by means of calling to overthrow the government, but to overthrow the community which is not coming. A community which forgets what an act of forcing to extremes means, because it does not know what role punctuation has anymore, and it does not know when and where to put a full stop to events that are beyond questioning, beyond negotiation, and beyond any other kind of settlement. When Emanuel greets Mallarmé and other French writers, while bidding goodbye to American poets such as Walt Whitman on the grounds that she fell in love with capitalism because of commas (40), she lets her speaker embody not only a lost America, but also an America which can be recuperated on the ground of that very loss, of nothingness, and silence. As if recalling the voice of another ghost, who also speaks from beyond the pulverized image of America, Allen Ginsberg, Emanuel intimates by imitating:

> America, you don't need poetry.
> Could we not go back to the way things were:
>
> a page that once lay as bare as moon
> above the black lapping of leaves?
>
> Before you were a link in my chain, before I was
> money for your tolls?
>
> Before you and I were forced to speak? (42)

What must be forced to the extreme is the perennial question of speaking what and on whose behalf. What subject position does the dog occupy? Can a dog's *wuf* become law? *Noose and Hook* powerfully suggests that a coming community is a community which sniffs properly at its superiors and thus unties its bands with objects that fall off the table.

COUNTER-MYTHOLOGIES

> *They know so much more, and so much less,*
> *"innocent details" and other.*
> —JOHN ASHBERY

> *When I was up against putting down the complete conception that I had gradually acquired by listening seeing feeling and experience, I was faced by the trouble that I had acquired all this knowledge gradually but when I had it I had it completely at one time. Now that may never have been a trouble to you but it was a terrible trouble to me.*
> —GERTRUDE STEIN

I have begun this book with the assumption that Emanuel's poems, by conjuring a tight proximity between the writer and the reader, have a specific political aim, namely to pulverize the image that ideological doctrines have, especially as they relate to the programmatic aspect of poetry. While attention has been given to the "mythologies of America" through individual readings that showed how some of these mythologies rest on decoding, misinterpreting, and reconstructing European portraits of thought, here, at the end, what must be emphasized, however, is also the aspect of the writer who takes pleasure in her craft.

Emanuel is not merely a political poet, nor merely fancifully a philosophical thinker, nor, finally a brilliant American cultural theorist, but a writer who understands words well. She knows the power of words. She knows what their discursive and aesthetic function and effect consist of. Writing, for Emanuel, can almost be said to be part of a larger epistemological quest, which, however, does not stand individually but is pushed towards converging with ontological ideas about how poems come into existence, what they can do to a reader's own background knowledge, and how they can widen the reader's perspective through specific cultural referencing. She is thus a poet interested in the methodology of creativity as an overall epistemic project. How to formulate into writing what you come to know is a concern that Emanuel takes on board and extends particularly from Gertrude Stein.

In her study, *Gertrude Stein: Woman without Qualities*, G.F. Mitrano asserts that what is specifically important for the depiction of portraits with words is taking stock of how knowledge acquisition (of things and others) occurs and over what period of time. As she puts it: "the problem of the gradual knowledge of others, and whether it can pass into writing, is a version of the question of truth in philosophy [...] writing is always a figure of knowing – its portrait" (Mitrano, 2006: 133). For Emanuel, this 'knowing' occurs in the grounding of subjectivity in craft. In other words, the challenge is to make explicitly public, or rather literally public that which is implicitly private. Whereas for Stein this project was achieved by means of formally dismantling the sentence, thus creating a poetics of syntactical and abstract essence, Emanuel allows the dismantled sentence to be re-constructed along the lines of a poetics of cultural creativity. On Stein's portraits, and the desire to see the portrait "as exemplary of a writing open to externality," Mitrano further adds that "the portrait impacts on us as a moment of knowing rather than representation" (133). This moment of openness of writing through the visual impact is for Emanuel a moment of representation that continuously becomes a depiction of knowing the thing in itself (*an sich*). The culture of the thing is not only to take 'the thing' literally, but at the same time also to think about it.

I have also suggested that although Emanuel is consistent in her critique of literalism, her own poems can be read quite literally. Her depiction of portraits, whether of writers, actors, philosophers, or unskilled others, can be seen against the background of a desire to be as inclusive and non-prejudiced as possible. It is thus never an accident of failed imagery when the depictions of Gertrude Stein, for instance, invite more to a catachrestic rather than symbolic reading. Comical relief is achieved, to be sure, when one imagines Stein as a typewriter with a dress, but for Emanuel, neither the typewriter nor the dress is there merely for artificial purpose. What Emanuel does is speak the language of the objects. Speaking the language of inarticulate beings is remarkable and innovative also from the point of view of the critic who desires to assess her 'Americanness' against the background of an European legacy in terms of aesthetics and history of ideas.

But one cannot be mistaken. Emanuel's Americanness consists of America itself. This can be seen in the way in which she insists on continuing the line of the poetic thought of the most iconic of the American poets, such as Walt Whitman, Allen Ginsberg, Frank O'Hara, and John Ashbery. These poets are at their best when they embody America. As America, having become America, one can see what is wrong with America, what America is, from within. And it starts with taking the clothes off America. Whitman suggested it, Ginsberg did, O'Hara paraded its nakedness and Ashbery approved. Emanuel's work taken together is a feast of celebrating the poet, not in all the poet's glory, but in all the poet's naked vulnerability. America is great when America is naked. Even Gertrude Stein can be seen as part of the American poets whose strategy of transcending America is by stripping. Emanuel can't make herself suggest that Gertrude Stein may have entertained such an idea, quite literally, but the fact that we get to have Stein's dress associated with her typewriter rather than her body leaves room for imagining some other scenario. For Emanuel, as for the others mentioned here, the body is the last object to love beyond its submission to discursive powers. It is remarkable to note how Emanuel moves from the language of the body as inscribed by diction in *Hotel Fiesta,* to the language of the body as a relic in *The Dig.* In *Then Suddenly—* we have a shift again to the language of the body as self-conscious diction, which then culminates in the language of the body as inscribed by pure subversive linguistic hybridity in *Noose and Hook.* The body talks many things in Emanuel. And the reader gets the distinct impression that, for Emanuel, the aim of the poet is to attend to these things that are articulated each in their own particular and special way. The aim of the poet is to stand as a guard, watching.

Hotel Fiesta ends with the poem entitled: "The Poet in the Garret in America" and we read lines that unambiguously indicate what it means to want to escape representation but realize that such a desire is impossible. What remains is the vocative: "America!," the poet exclaims, thus evoking a whole tradition of invoking America continued by poets whose best cry also consisted of this direct address, as if wanting to say: *America, what's wrong with you, snap out of whatever it is that ails you! America, I love you forever!* Thus writes Emanuel, in prose that is more beautiful than the suggested clichés here, which, however, although clichés, can also be said to constitute the most moving moments in anyone's lives:

> I come up here to be disembodied and abstract,
> To feel the sycamore astir against my naked psyche.
> [...] America, I want to transcend you.
> Like this cardinal in the sycamore I love
> My own beautiful sensibility and have come here
> To be issued an invitation as exact and stunning
> As Eve's was in her green, frail, and sacramental
> World. Under all my winsome diction, you and I
> Are standing toe to toe, the diurnal, the divine.
> America, I am still hopeful and a woman of my time.
> (Emanuel, 1995: 119)

The poet who utters these words is not a simpleton, but one who knows how to construe an allegory of the way in which she loves America, actually as a romantic romance permeated with French sophistication. Such prophetic tone still reverberates with even more force in the subsequent works. In *The Dig*, "We, the Poets of America" proclaim what it is that one deals with here, in America, namely with the good and the bad as the *donnée*, the special gift of both/and:

> We are like you, America,
> when you were a rough draft,
> a marsh, a swamp, newt and savannah.
> [...] We have come to point out all

> your mistakes chalked blurrily
> on the beyond's blurry slates,
>
> to tell you that you're a blot and hell
> is vacant, dirty, dark and that there's
> nothing for miles but tragedy and grief
> and a squad of girls like us with which
> to spend eternity, dusting the infernal dust. (40-41)

Emanuel is not kidding when she takes it upon herself to instruct. And how lucky the ones who let themselves be instructed. In the poem "In English in a Poem" from *Then Suddenly—*, she thus says:

> I am giving a lecture on poetry
> to the painters who creak like saddles
> in their black leather jackets; in the studio,
> where a fire is burning like a painting of
> a fire, I am explaining my current work
> on the erotics of narrative.
> [...] Gertrude Stein said America
> was a *space filled with moving*, but I hate being moving.
> If you want to *feel*, go to the movies, because poetry
> has not intention of being moving; it is perhaps one
> of the few things left in America that is not moving.
> And yet, I am a fatalist when it comes to art
> and orgasm in English, because in English
> even a simile is a story and there is no trip
> so predictable that some poem won't take it.
> And just as I am finishing my lecture, here
> is the snowy hem of the end of the page
> and one of the painters says to me, "Actually,
> I found that very moving. Get in the car.
> I'll drive you home." (Emanuel, 1999: 60-61)

Emanuel on a lecture tour through America, making sure to pass on some wisdom and words of beauty to the unenlightened is a powerful image. Especially as one imagines that all this has taken place in actual fact. The title poem "Then Suddenly—" from *Then Suddenly—* surely indicates this much, as it sends shivers down the spine at the moment when the speaker in the poem addresses the cowboys of America, who know nothing, are unsophisticated and say "*garsh* a lot." She shouts at them: "get a life," but then this demand returns as an echo, and she hears the call herself:

> "Get a life in another world, because this is
> a page as bare and smooth as a bowling alley,"
> and then, suddenly – renouncing all matter –
> I am gone, and all that's left is a voice, soaring,
> invisible, disembodied, gobbling up the landscape,
> an airborne cloud of selfhood giving a poetry reading
> in which, Reader, I have made our paths cross! (62-63)

The careful reader will recognize that, indeed, after such a *tour de force*, the line in Emanuel's next work, *Noose and Hook*, "America, you don't need poetry" (42) calls for something more complex. What America needs is not words, but devotion, as devotion is beyond judgement.

Culminating thus with *Noose and Hook*, Emanuel has succeeded in being true to her own agenda as a writer who makes political and pleasurable gestures at once, namely by persisting in the myth of her own American anonymity, as intimated in her address to the Poetry Society of America (referred to in the introduction). The other aim expressed in such a manifesto was to show that as an American 'anonymous' writer, she is a writer who is not only able to confront the gaze of the antropomorphized grave that she digs for herself, but also speak its language. What does speaking the language of digs and dogs mean, one might ask, for the understanding of the significance of placing a cornerstone on top of an edifice made out of pulverized pebbles? And yet, what else would hold "secrets," "privacy," "deposits of the inarticulate and incomprehensible," "the queer," "the recherché," "the national?" would Emanuel answer, thus posing another question in return, but one which is not merely rhetorical.

These key notions can be said to represent part of Emanuel's project of formulating a poetry of becoming. What is new, however, and what sets Emanuel apart from other American contemporary poets who shift between epistemological and existential concerns is the fact that her questioning movement from: 'how do I know this world of which I am part?, or 'who am I in this world?,' goes back to earlier forms of representation, prior to the separation of aesthetics from science.

Emanuel's pulverized portraits suggest a return to a Shakespearean approach: *how can I know thee? — You can't,* one can imagine Shakespeare answering back. And this is good enough for Emanuel. It is here, in this unintended search for knowledge that her poems display a multifaceted evaluation of the multiple significations that such words as "the secret," "privacy," "the incomprehensible," "the queer," and "the recherché" can hold for the reader who reads with dust in her eyes. For Emanuel, the poetry of becoming is the poetry of knowing by sensing; the poetry of knowing what it does know that it knows.

The pulverized portraits of poetry and poets alike are thus 'eradicated' mythologies against whose background the following propositional demand emerges: that any ontology must first be a style, and any epistemology must first be poetic.

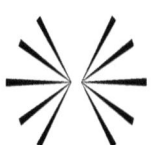

REFERENCES

Agamben, Giorgio (1993). *The Coming Community.* Trans. Michael Hardt. Minneapolis: University of Minnesota Press.

—— (1993b). *Stanzas: Word and Phantasm in Western Culture.* Trans. Ronald L. Martinez. Minneapolis: University of Minnesota Press.

—— (1995). *The Idea of Prose.* Trans. Michael Sullivan and Sam Whitsitt. Albany: SUNY Press.

—— (1999). *Potentialities.* Trans. Daniel Heller-Roazen. Stanford: Stanford University Press.

—— (1999b). *The End of the Poem: Studies in Poetics.* Trans. Daniel Heller-Roazen. Stanford: Stanford University Press.

—— (1999c). *The Man Without Content* (Meridian: Crossing Aesthetics). Stanford: Stanford University Press.

—— (2000). *Means Without End: Notes on Politics* (Theory Out of Bounds). Trans Vincenzo Binetti & Cesare Casarino. Minneapolis: University of Minnesota Press.

—— (2002). *Homo Sacer: Sovereign Power and Bare Life.* Trans. Daniel Heller-Roazen. Stanford: Stanford University Press.

—— (2004). *The Open: Man and Animal.* Trans. Kevin Attell. Stanford: Stanford University Press.

Arnold, Andrew (2002). "At Lest, a Heppy Lend." *TIME.comix on Krazy Kat.* Posted Tuesday, Mar. 19, 2002 [http://www.time.com/time/columnist/arnold/article/0,9565,218816,00.html].

Ashbery, John (1981). *Shadow Train. Paradoxes and Oxymorons.* New York: The Viking Press.

Ashbery, John (1991). *Reported Sightings. Art Chronicles 1957–1987.* Cambridge Massachusetts: Harvard University Press.

Baudelaire, Charles (1968). *Baudelaire: Œuvres complètes.* Paris: Seuil.

Bell, Mark (1997). *Aphorism in the Francophone Novel of the Twentieth Century.* Montreal & Kingston: McGill-Queen's University Press.

Berman, Avis (1993). "Rediscovering Akiba Emanuel." *Alexander Gallery Catalogue.* Exhibition: May 5-June 15, 1994, New York.

Bos, Réne ten (2005). "On the Possibility of Formless Life: Agamben's Politics of the Gesture." *Ephemera: Theory of Politics in Organization* 5 (1): 26-44.

Bush, M. L. (1991). "'Up for the Commonweal:' The Significance of Tax Grievances in the English Rebellions of 1536." *English Historical Review.* Vol. 106, No. 419 Apr. pp. 299-318.

Butler, Samuel (1979). *Prose Observations.* (Oxford English Texts) Oxford: Oxford University Press

Carlyle, Thomas (1827). "Jean Paul Friedrich Richter." *Critical Miscellaneous Essays Collected and Republished by Thomas Carlyle in Four Volumes.* Vol. 1. Boston: Brown and Taggard MDCCCLX.

Clark, Timothy (1997). *The Theory of Inspiration.* Manchester and New York: Manchester University Press.

Cole, John R. (1992). *The Olympian Dream and Youthful Rebellion of Rene Descartes.* Urbana and Chicago: University of Illinois Press.

Coleridge, Samuel Taylor (1836). *Specimens of the table talk of the late Samuel Taylor Coleridge.* Ed. Henry Nelson Coleridge. Harper & Brothers.

Crawford, Robert (2001). *The Modern Poet: Poetry, Academia, and Knowledge since the 1750s.* Oxford: Oxford University Press.

Cronkite, Walter (1935/2009). "Daily Texan talks Great Depression with author." *Daily Texan Online.* [http://www.dailytexanonline.com/walter-cronkite/daily-texan-talks-great-depression-with-author-1.1775552]. Original run date: March 22, 1935.

Cook, Jon (2004). *Poetry in Theory. An Anthology 1900-2000.* Oxford: Blackewell Publishing.

De Zegher, Catherine, ed. et al. (2000). *Untitled Passages by Henri Michaux.* London and New York: Merrell Publishers.

Delville, Michel (1998). *The American Prose Poem: Poetic Form and the Boundaries of Genre.* Gainesville: University Press of Florida.

Derrida, Jacques (1974). *Of Grammatology.* Trans. Gayatri Spivak. Baltimore and London: The Johns Hopkins University Press.

―――― (1981). "Title (to be specified)." *Sub-Stance* 31.

―――― (1987). *The Truth in Painting.* Trans. Geoff Bennington and Ian Mcleod. Chicago: The University of Chicago Press.

―――― (1998). *Limited Inc.* Trans. Samuel Weber. Evanston: Northwestern University Press.

Domangue, Camille (1997). "Ordinary Objects: Interview with Lynn Emanuel." AWP Chronicle. Sept. 1997.
[http://www.english.pitt.edu/people/emanuel/interview.html].

Edson, Russell (1964) *The Very Thing that Happens.* Norfolk CT: New Directions.

―――― (1982). "Portrait of the Writer as a Fat Man: Some Subjective Ideas or Notions on the Care and Feeding of Prose Poems." *Claims for Poetry.* Donald Hall, ed. Ann Arbor: University of Michigan.

Elias, Camelia (2004). *The Fragment: Towards a History and Poetics of a Performative Genre.* Bern: Peter Lang.

Elias, Camelia & Sørensen, Bent, eds. (2005). *Cultural Text Studies 1: An Introduction.* Aalborg: Aalborg University Press.

Elias, Camelia & Birch, Andrea, eds. (2006). *Cultural Text Studies 2: Transatlantic.* Aalborg: Aalborg University Press.

Emanuel, Lynn (1979). *Oblique Light.* Pittsburgh: Slow Loris Press.

―――― (1988). *The Technology of Love.* Abattoir Editions.

―――― (1994). *Film noir: train trip out of metropolis.* (Poem). The Antioch Review. June 22. Volume 52 Issue: n3 Page: p495 (1).

―――― (1995). *The Dig and Hotel Fiesta. Two Volumes of Poetry.* Urbana and Chicago: University of Illinois Press.

―――― (1999). *Then Suddenly–.* Pittsburgh: University of Pittsburgh Press.

—— (2002). *Lynn Emanuel: Self-Portrait with Words*. Printed letterpress by Fameorshame for the Center for Book Arts, New York.

—— (2006). *Dogge Songs*. Unpublished manuscript.

—— (2010). *Noose and Hook*. (Pitt Poetry Series). Pittsburgh: University of Pittsburgh Press.

—— "What is American About American Poetry?" *Poetry Society of America*. [http://www.poetrysociety.org/emanuel.html]. Last accessed 2010.

Fadiman, Clifton (1962). "Lec and the Art of the Aphorist." *Unkempt Thoughts*. Stanislaw Jerzy Lec. Trans. Jacek Galazka. New York: St Martin's Press.

Friebert, Stuart and Young, David (1985). *Models of the Universe: An Anthology of the Prose Poem*. Oberlin College Press.

Genette, Gerard (1987). *Paratexts: Thresholds of Interpretation*. Trans. Jane E. Lewin. Cambridge: Cambridge University Press.

Heffernan, James (1993). *Museum of Words – The Poetics of Ekphrasis from Homer to Ashbery*. Chicago and London: The University of Chicago Press.

Herzl, Theodor (1943). *The Jewish State: An Attempt at a Modern Solution of the Jewish Question*. Forward by Chaim Weizman. New York: Scopus Publishing Company.

Hinton, Laura and Hogue, Cynthia (2002). *We Who Love to be Astonished: Experimental Women's Writing and Performance Poetics*. Tuscaloosa, Alabama. University of Alabama Press.

Horvath, Brooke (1991). "Why the Prose Poem?" *Denver Quarterly* 25. pp.: 105-15.

—— (1992). "The Prose Poem and the Secret Life of Poetry." *American Poetry Review* Sept/Oct. pp.11-14.

Galvin, Rachel (2004). "Neither Heads nor Tails: The Middle province in Octavio Paz's Aguila o Sol?" *World Literature Today*. September-December.

Jabès, Edmond (1972). *The Book of Questions. Volume 1. The Book of Questions. The Book of Yukel. Return to the Book*. Trans. Rosmarie Waldrop. Hanover and London: Wesleyan University Press.

Jones, Gavin (1999). *Strange Talk: The Politics of Dialect Literature in Gilded Age America*. Berkeley and Los Angeles: University of California Press.

Joyce, James (1992). *Ulysses*. London: Penguin Groups.

Kafka, Franz (1971). *The Complete Works of Franz Kafka*. New York: Schoken.

Lehman, David, ed. (2003). *Great American Prose Poems: From Poe to the Present*. New York: Scribner Poetry.

Lethem, Jonathan, ed. (2000). "Introduction." *The Vintage Book of Amnesia: An Anthology of Writing on the Subject of Memory Loss*. New York: Vintage Books.

Litowitz, Douglas (2000). "Gramsci, Hegemony, and the Law." 2000 *Brigham Young University Law Review* 515.

Lotman, Y.M. & Uspensky, B.A. (1978). "On the Semiotic Mechanism of Culture." *New Literary History*, Vol. IX, No. 2, Winter 211-232.

McGurl, Mark (2009). *The Program Era. Postwar Fiction and the Rise of Creative Writing*. Cambridge: Harvard University Press.

Michaux, Henri (1963) *Henri Michaux*. Trans. John Ashbery. London: Robert Fraser Gallery.

Monroe, Jonathan (1987). *A Poverty of Objects: The Prose Poem and the Politics of Genre*. Ithaca NY: Cornell University Press.

Monte, Steven (2000). *Invisible Fences*. Lincoln & London: University of Nebraska Press.

Nietzsche, Friedrich (1954). *The Portable Nietzsche*. Trans. Walter Kaufmann. Toronto: Penguin Books. Viking Penguin Inc.

―――― (1990). *The Twilight of the Idols and The Anti-Christ: or How to Philosophize with a Hammer*. London: Penguin Classics

Preminger, Alex, ed. (1965). *Encyclopedia of Poetry and Poetics*. Princeton, N.J.: Princeton University Press.

Riffaterre, Michael (1983). "On the Prose Poem's Formal Features". *The Prose Poem in France: Theory and Practice*. Eds. Mary Ann Caws and Hermine Riffaterre. New York: Columbia University Press.

Rosmarin, Adena (1986). *The Power of Genre*. Minneapolis: University of Minnesota Press.

Schmitt, Carl (1924/1988). *The Crisis of Parliamentary Democracy.* Trans. Ellen Kennedy. The MIT Press.

Simic, Charles (2003). *The Metaphysician in the Dark.* Ann Harbor: the University to Michigan Press.

Slinn, E. Warwick (1999). "Poetry and Culture: Performativity & Critique." *New Literary History.* Vol. 30, No. 1 Winter 1999.

Stein, Gertrude (1962). *Selected Writings of Gertrude Stein.* Ed. with an introduction and notes by Carl van Vechten and with an essay on Gertrude Stein by F. W. Dupee. New York: The Modern Library.

────── (1967). *Look at me now and here I am: Writings and Lectures 1911-1945.* Eds. Patricia Meyerowitz, and Elizabeth Sprigge. London: Penguin Books.

────── (1975). *How to Write.* New York: Dover Publications, Inc.

────── (1995). *The Making of Americans.* Chicago: Dalkey Archive Press.

Steiner, George (1971). *In Bluebeard's Castle: Some Notes toward the Redefinition of Culture.* New Haven, Conn.: Yale University Press.

Svalina, Mathias (2002). "An Interview with Lynn Emanuel." *Blackbird: An Online Journal of Literature and the Arts.* Fall 2000, Vol. 1 No. 2. [http://www.blackbird.vcu.edu/v1n2/features/emanuel_l_021403/emanuel_l_text.htm].

Suárez Araúz, Nicomedes (1984). "The Amnesis Manifesto" [http://www.smith.edu/calc/amnesia/manifesto.html]

Upton, Lee (1993). "Structural Politics: The Prose Poetry of Russell Edson." *South Atlantic Review.* Vol. 58. No. 4, Nov. pp. 101-115.

Verdicchio, Massimo & Burch, Robert, eds. (2002). *Between Philosophy and Poetry: Writing, Rhythm, History.* London: Continuum, Athlone Press.

Wagner, Peter, ed. (1996). *Icons – Texts – Iconotexts: Essays on Ekphrasis and Intermediality.* Berlin & New York: Walter de Gruyter.

Williams, Tyrone (2002). *C.C.* San Francisco: Krupskaya.

Zawinski, Andrena (year undisclosed). "Poetry in Review". In *Posse Review. Osiduy.* Issue 9. Vol. 1 [http://webdelsol.com/InPosse/zawinski9.htm].

ABOUT THE AUTHOR

Camelia Elias is an associate professor of American Studies at Roskilde University, Denmark. She has published a book on the concept of fragment, and another on the gaze in feminist, queer, and postcolonial films. She has also edited books within cultural studies, poetry criticism, and a special volume on the work of Raymond Federman. Currently she is working on a book length project on epistemologies of creative writing. Apart from academic work, she writes prose poetry and makes art.

www.ingramcontent.com/pod-product-compliance
Lightning Source LLC
Chambersburg PA
CBHW022010160426
43197CB00007B/358